Introduction to Coloring in Reverse.

Coloring in reverse provides a place for peaceful, open reflection.

In a world that seems to demand a constant state of high arousal bordering on anxiety, giving ourself time for calm, open exploration has never been more crucial to our wellbeing.

Simply place your pen down on one of our original designs and let your mind do the rest.

Relax, there is no goal or finishing line here, and that's okay.

BLANK PAGE

HELLO, I AM YOUR FIRST BLANK PAGE.

Questions for Pause.

You will notice throughout this book that there are blank pages with some open questions on them. Like the one on the left here.

These are asked to invite you to pause for a moment if you'd like. You can also use the blank page or another coloring page to explore an answer further. There are no right or wrong ways to approach this book.

Remember there is no rush, it is okay to enjoy the process with no end goal in sight.

Straight lines or squiggly lines, all are welcome here.

BLANK PAGE

WHEN DO YOU FEEL MOST AT PEACE?

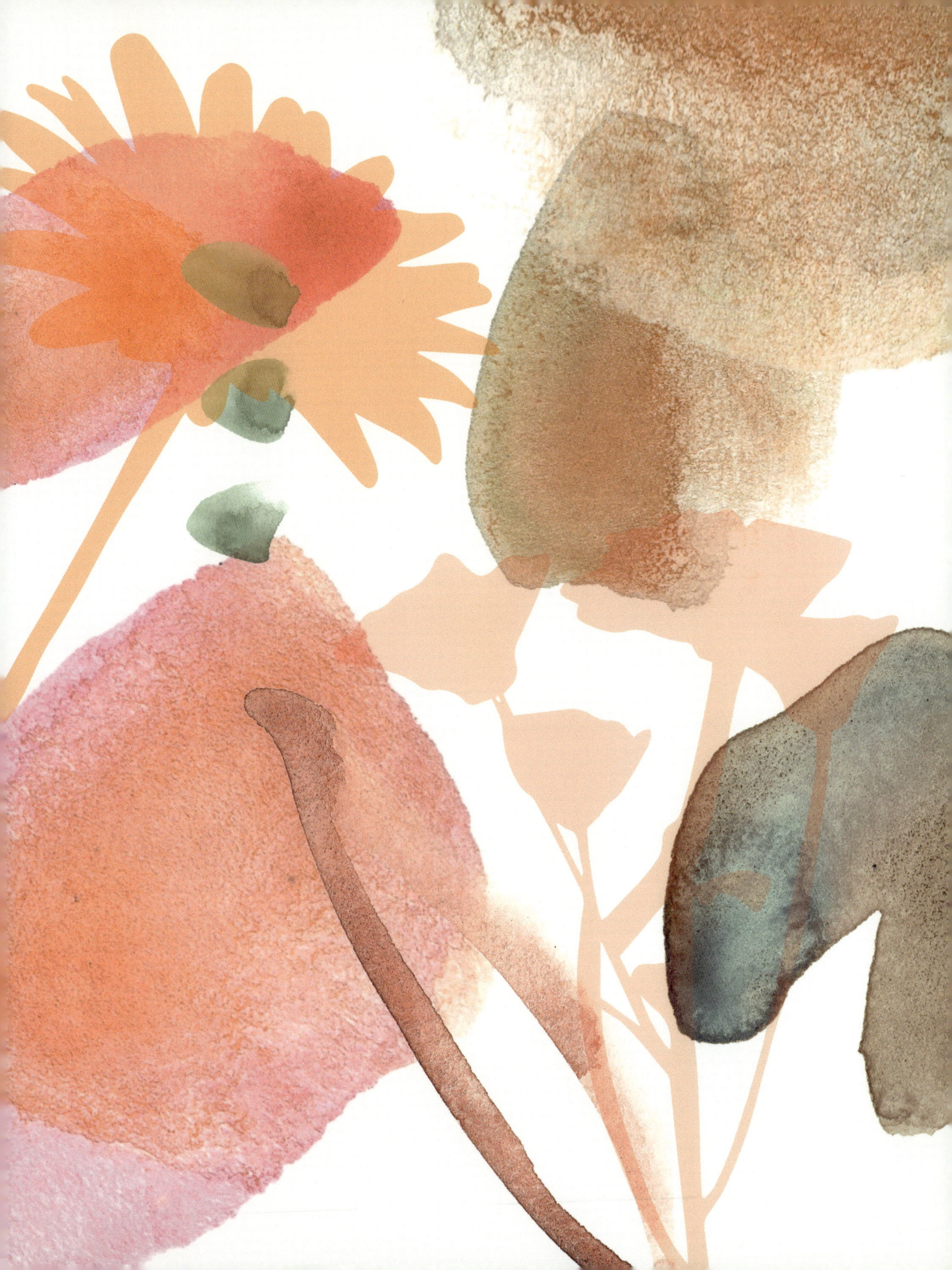

BLANK PAGE

WHAT HAVE YOU OVERCOME IN YOUR LIFE?

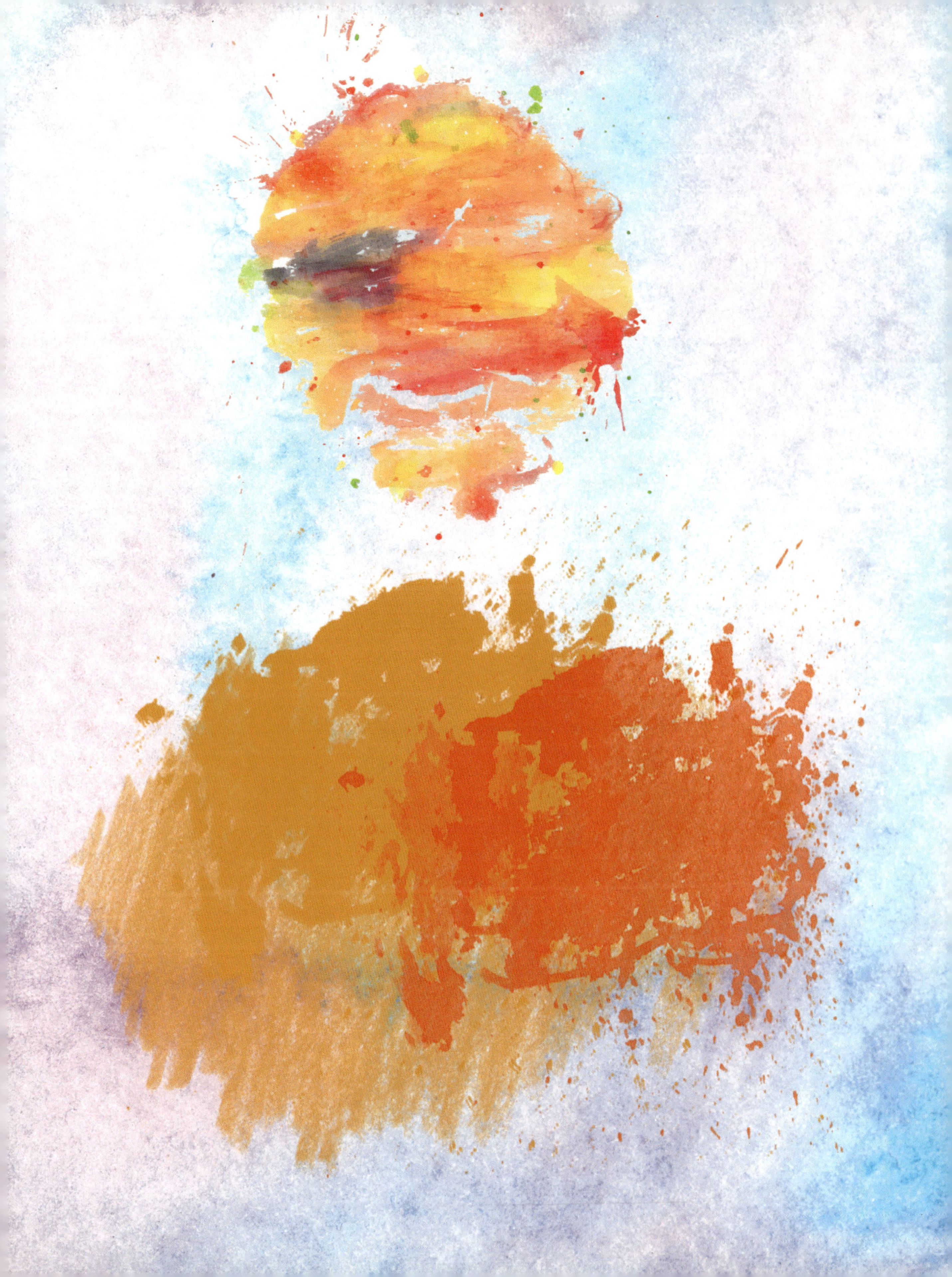

BLANK PAGE

WHAT DOES PEACE LOOK LIKE TO YOU?

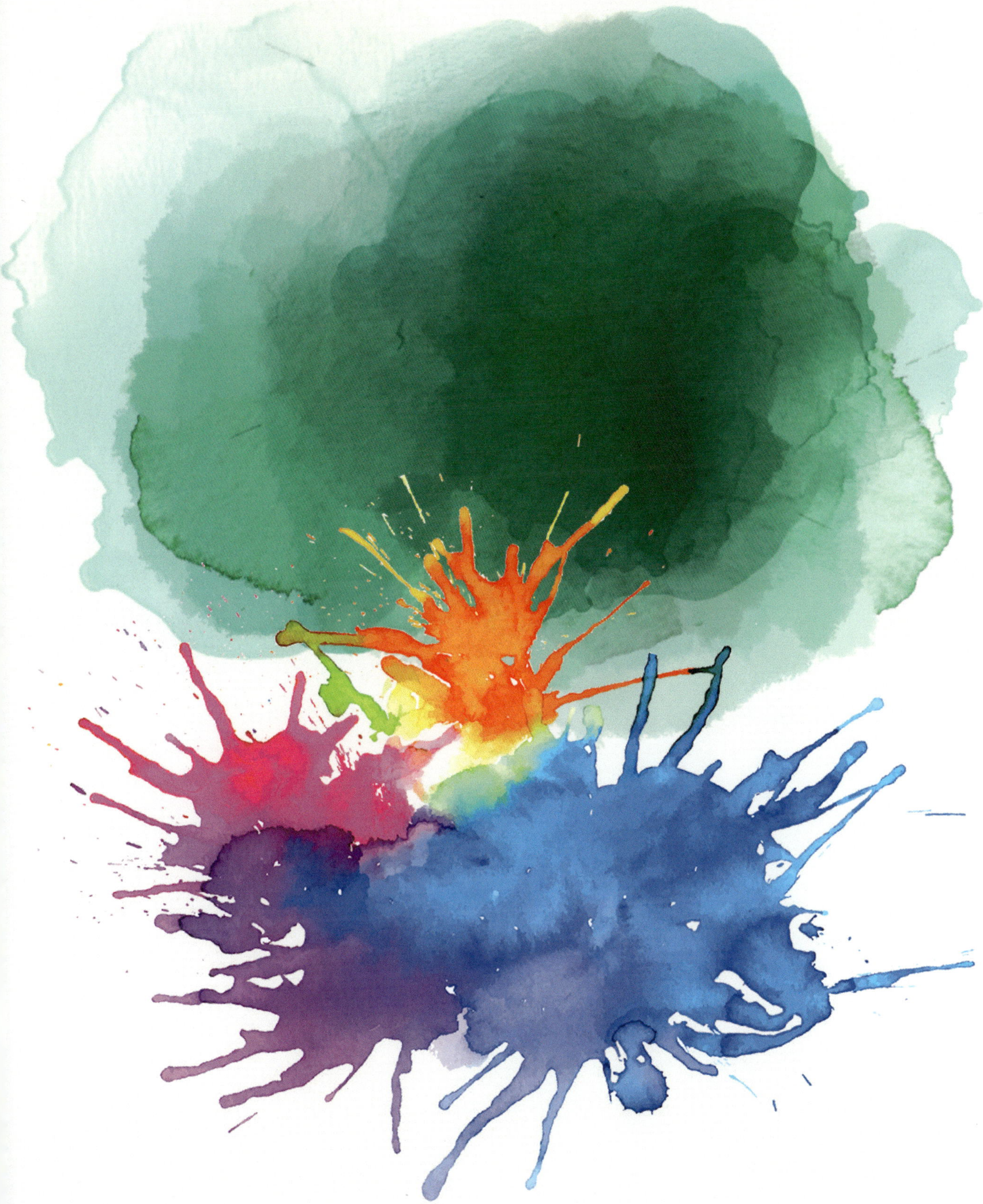

BLANK PAGE

HOW WELL DO YOU KNOW YOURSELF?

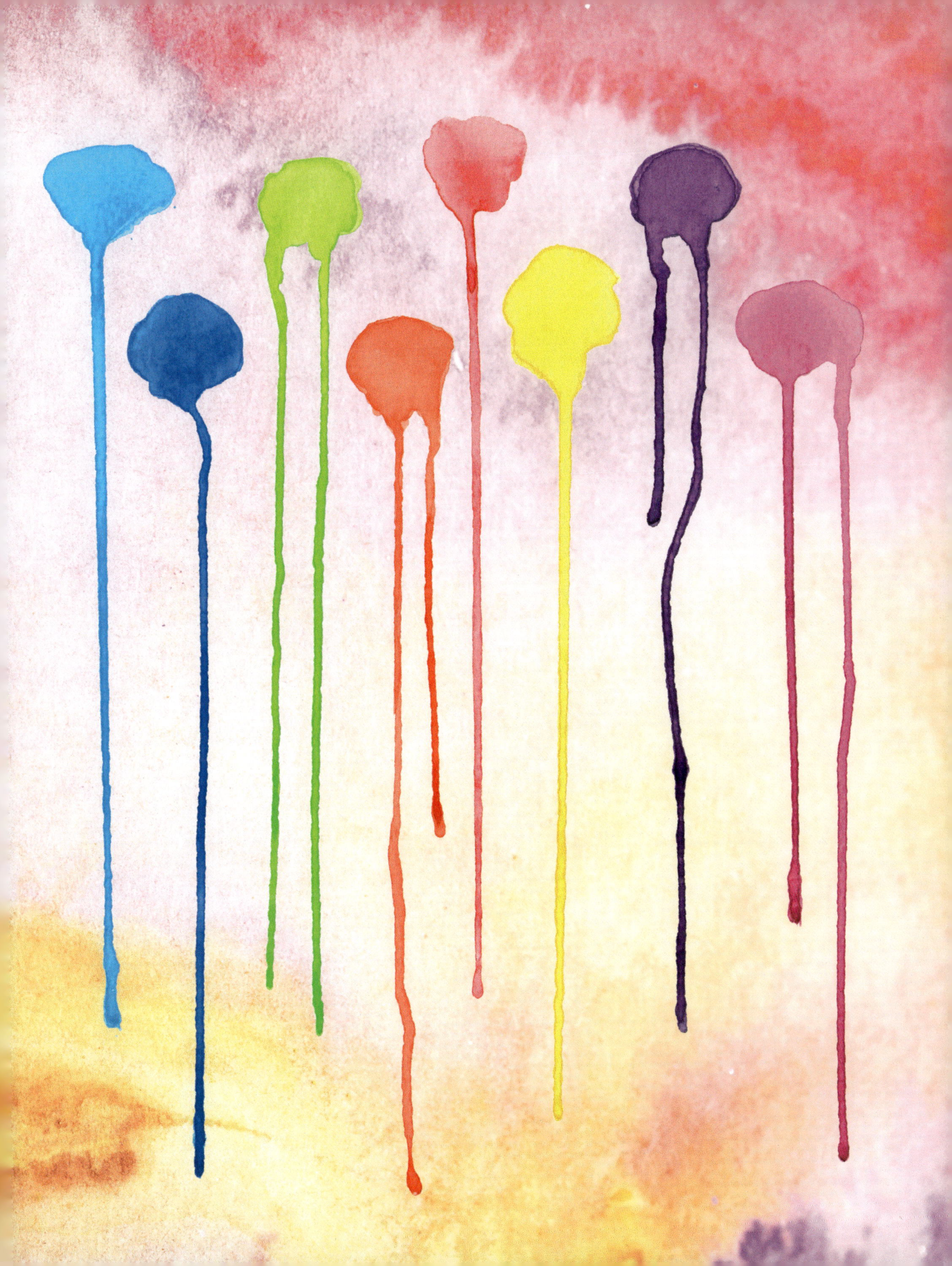

BLANK PAGE

CAN YOU IMAGINE THE SPACE BETWEEN YOUR EYES?

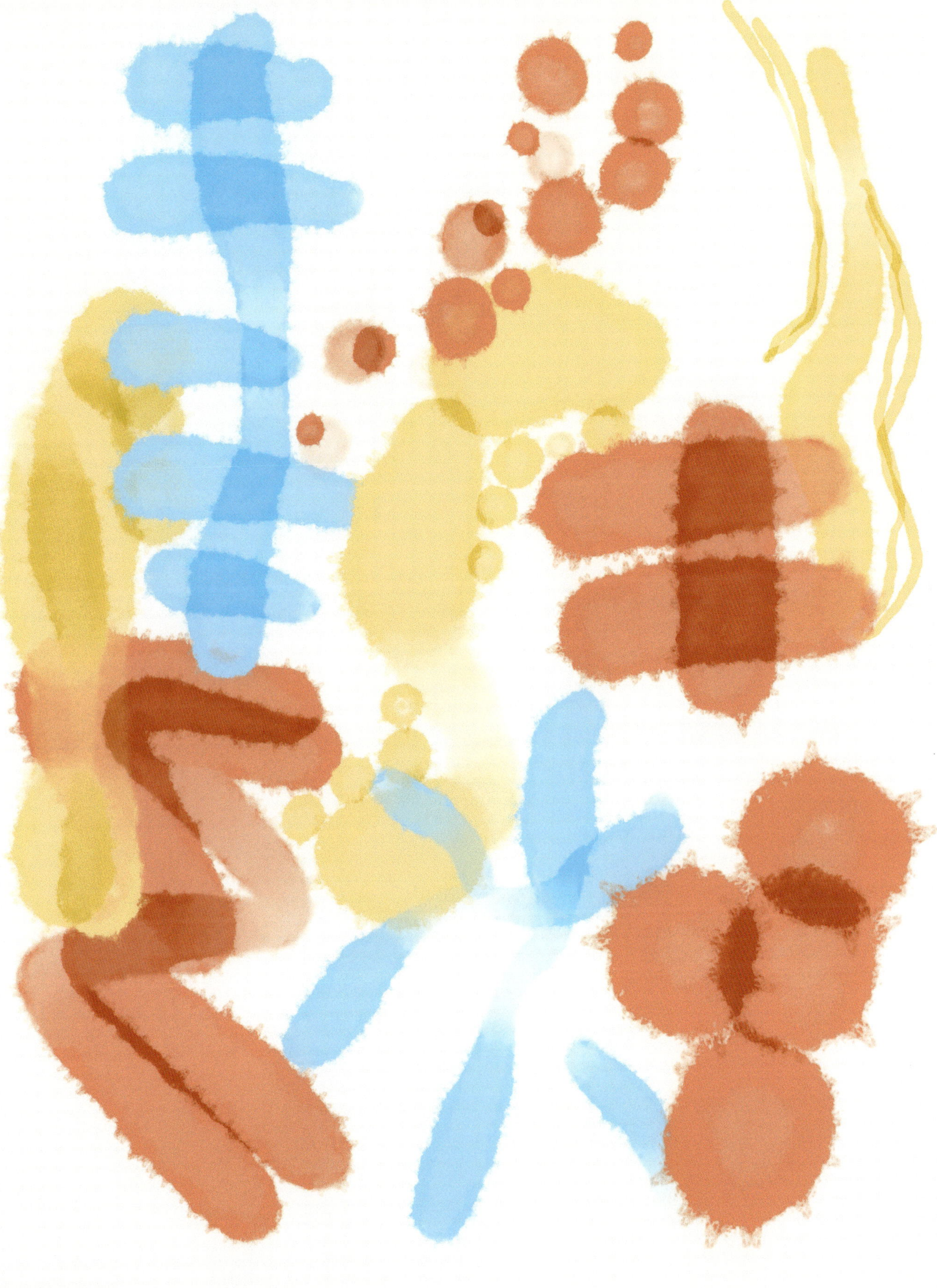

BLANK PAGE

WHEN DO YOU FEEL MOST SAFE?

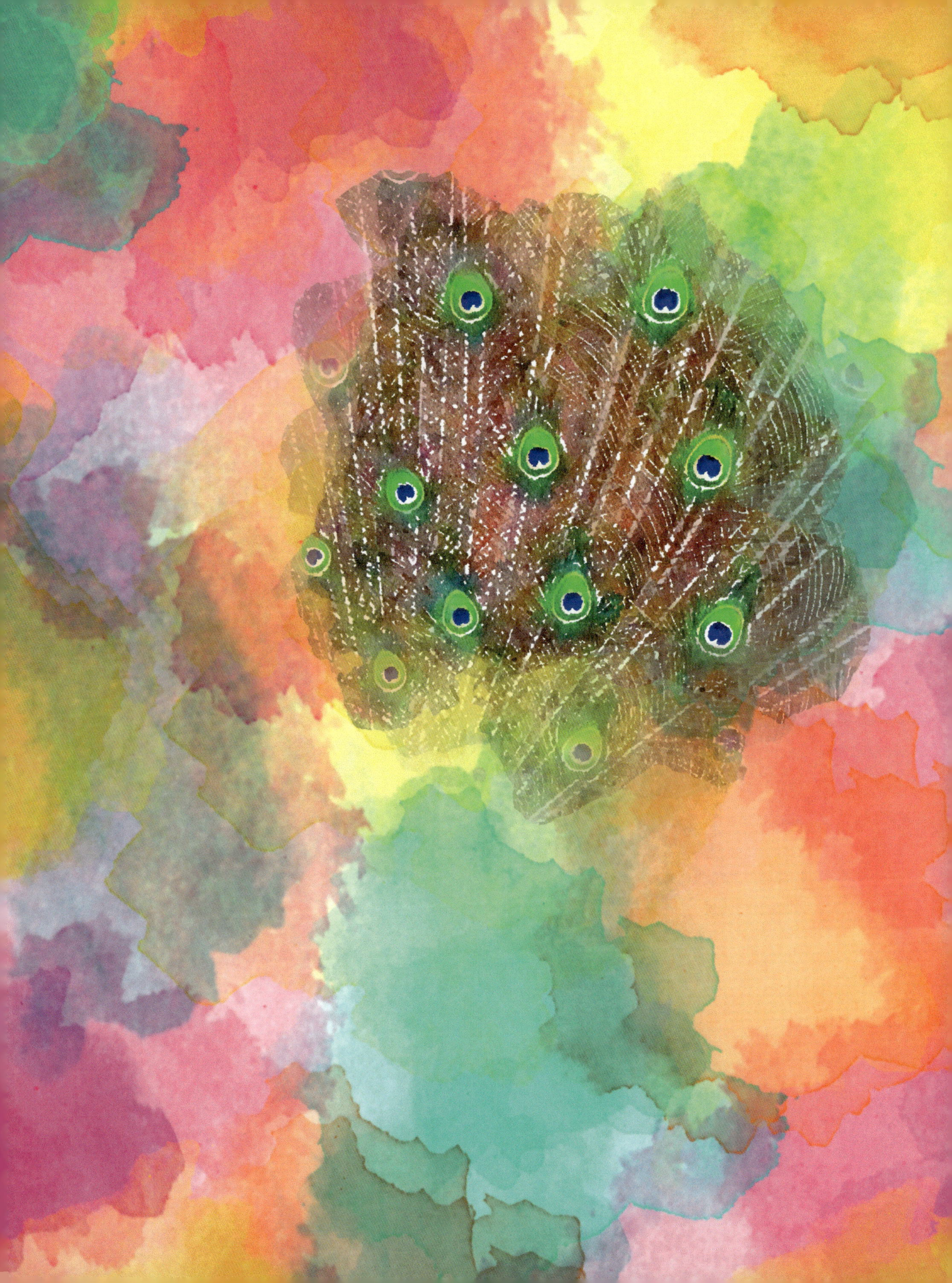

BLANK PAGE

WHAT DO YOU SEE WHEN YOU LOOK IN THE MIRROR?

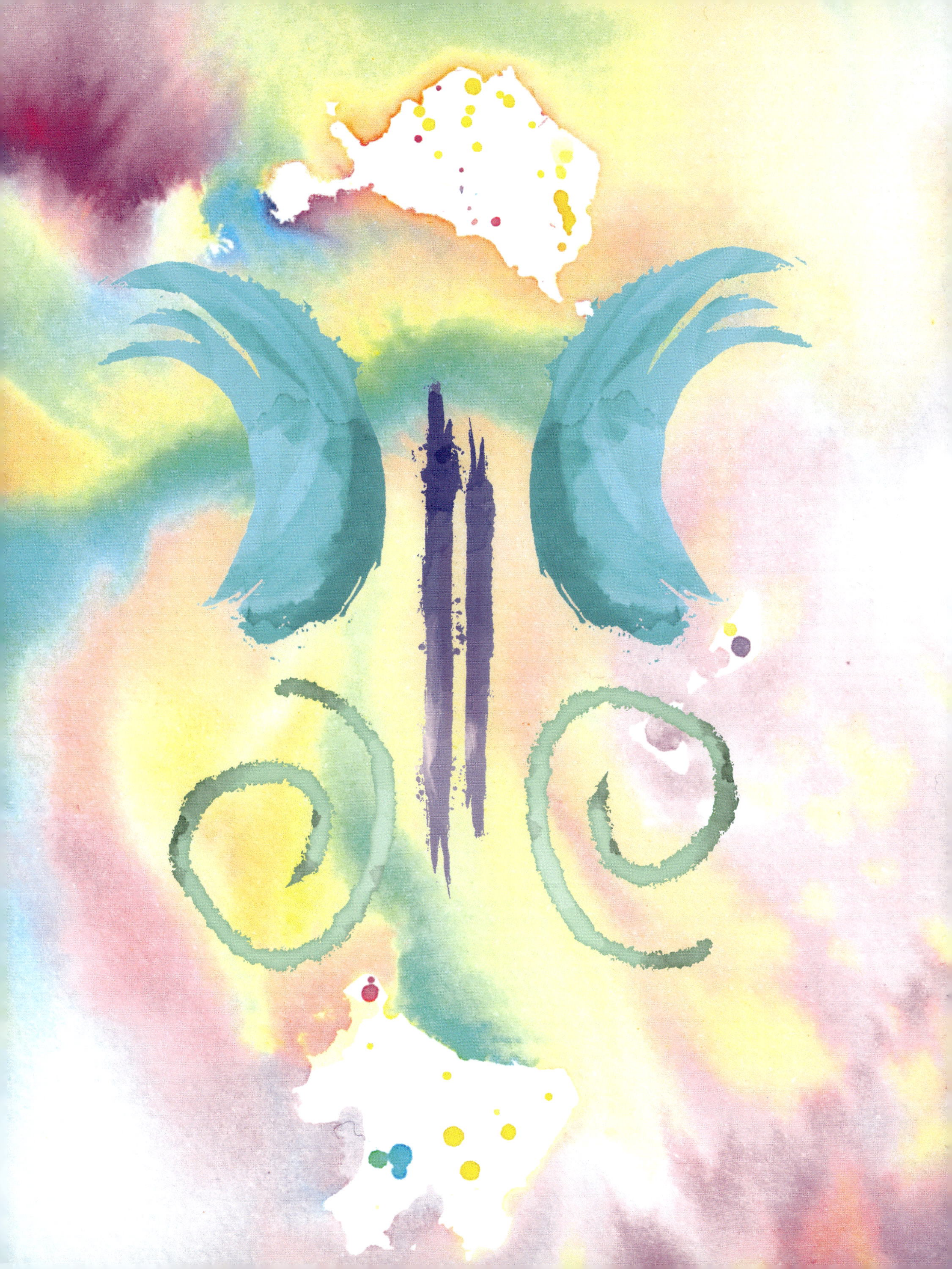

BLANK PAGE

CAN YOU IMAGINE THE SPACE BETWEEN YOUR SHOULDERS?

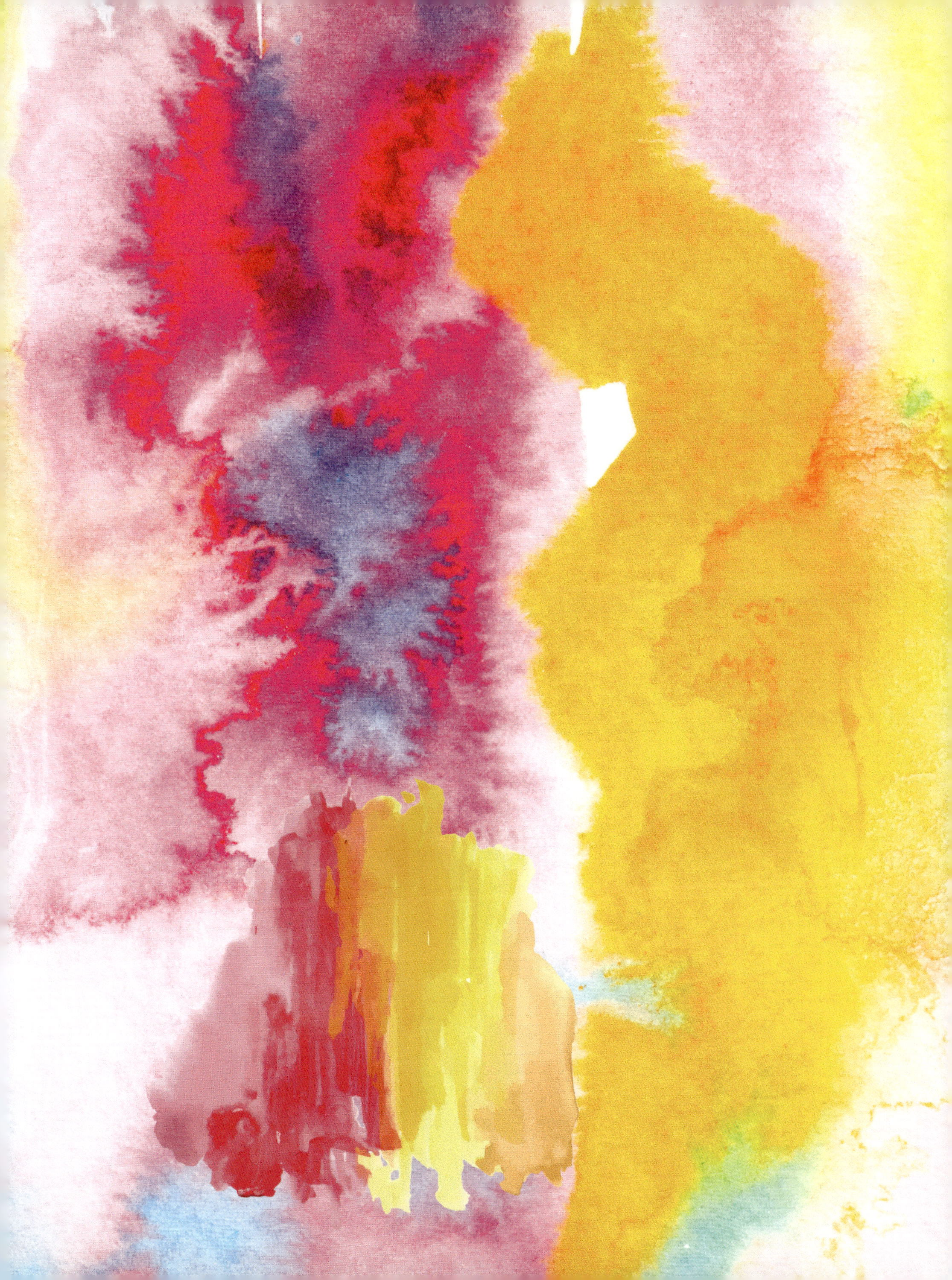

BLANK PAGE

DO YOU HAVE A FAVOURITE SHAPE TO DRAW?

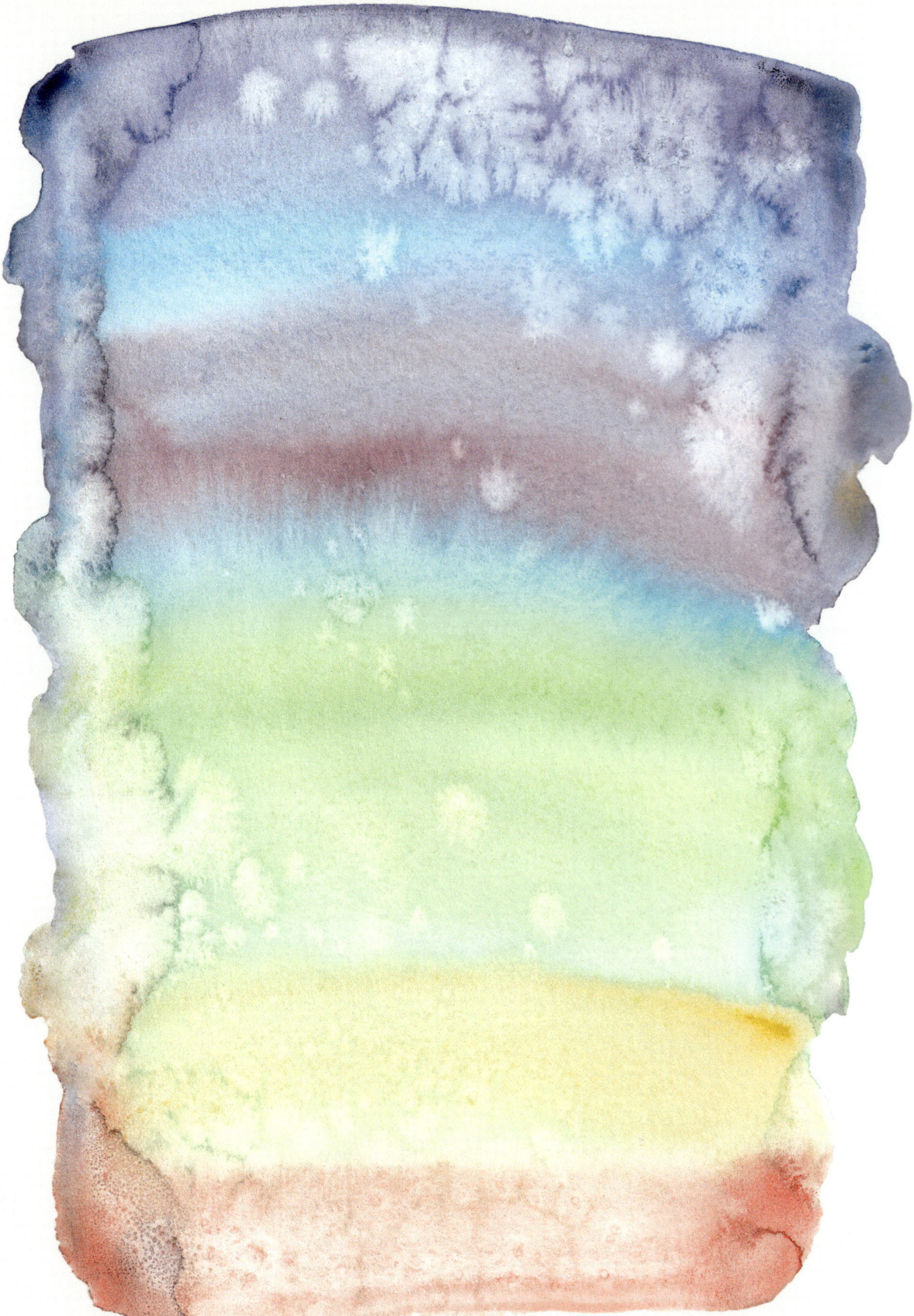

BLANK PAGE

WHAT DO YOU FEAR THE MOST?

BLANK PAGE

WHAT IS LOVE TO YOU?

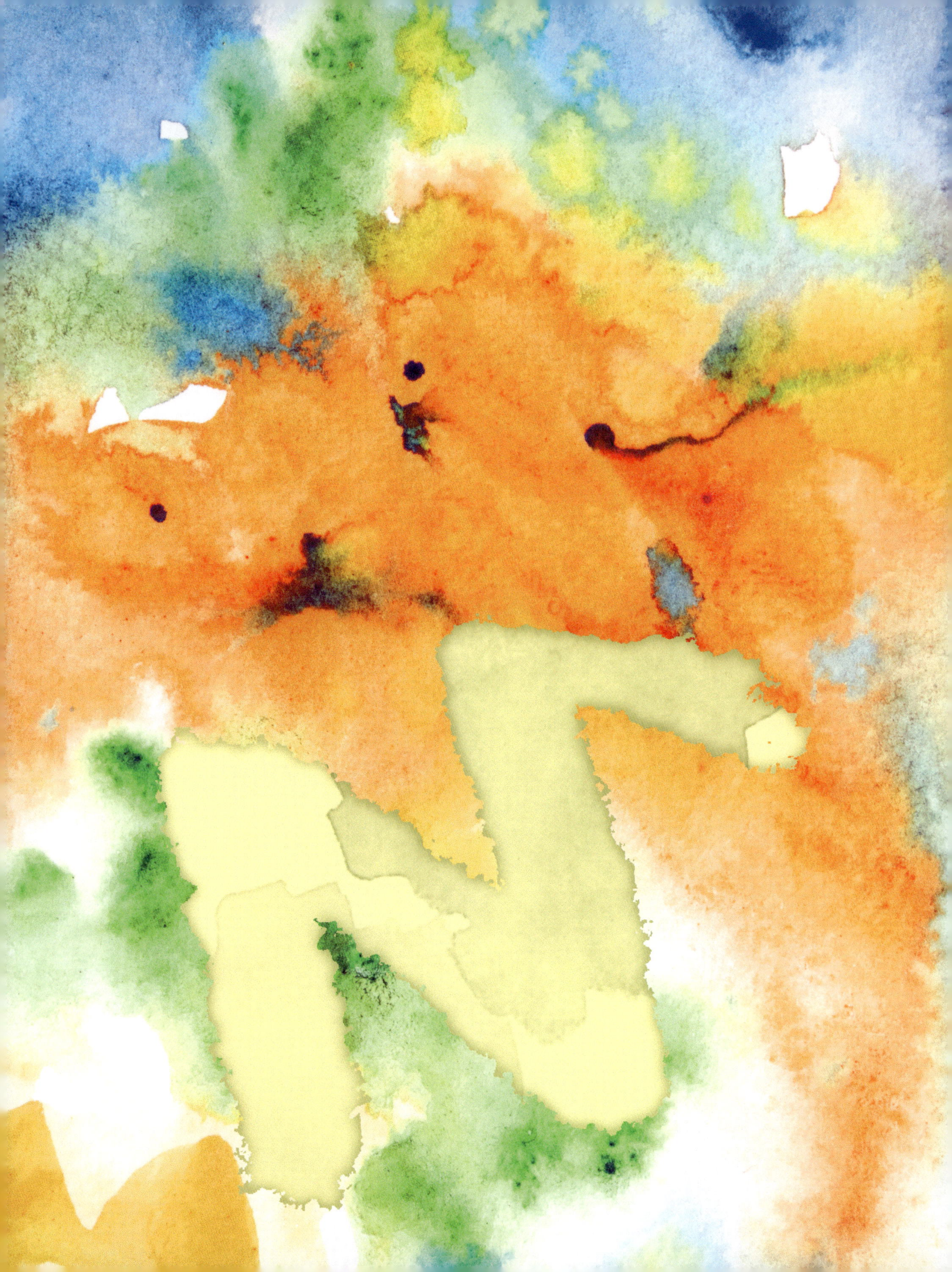

BLANK PAGE

WHAT DO YOU HOPE FOR IN THE FUTURE?

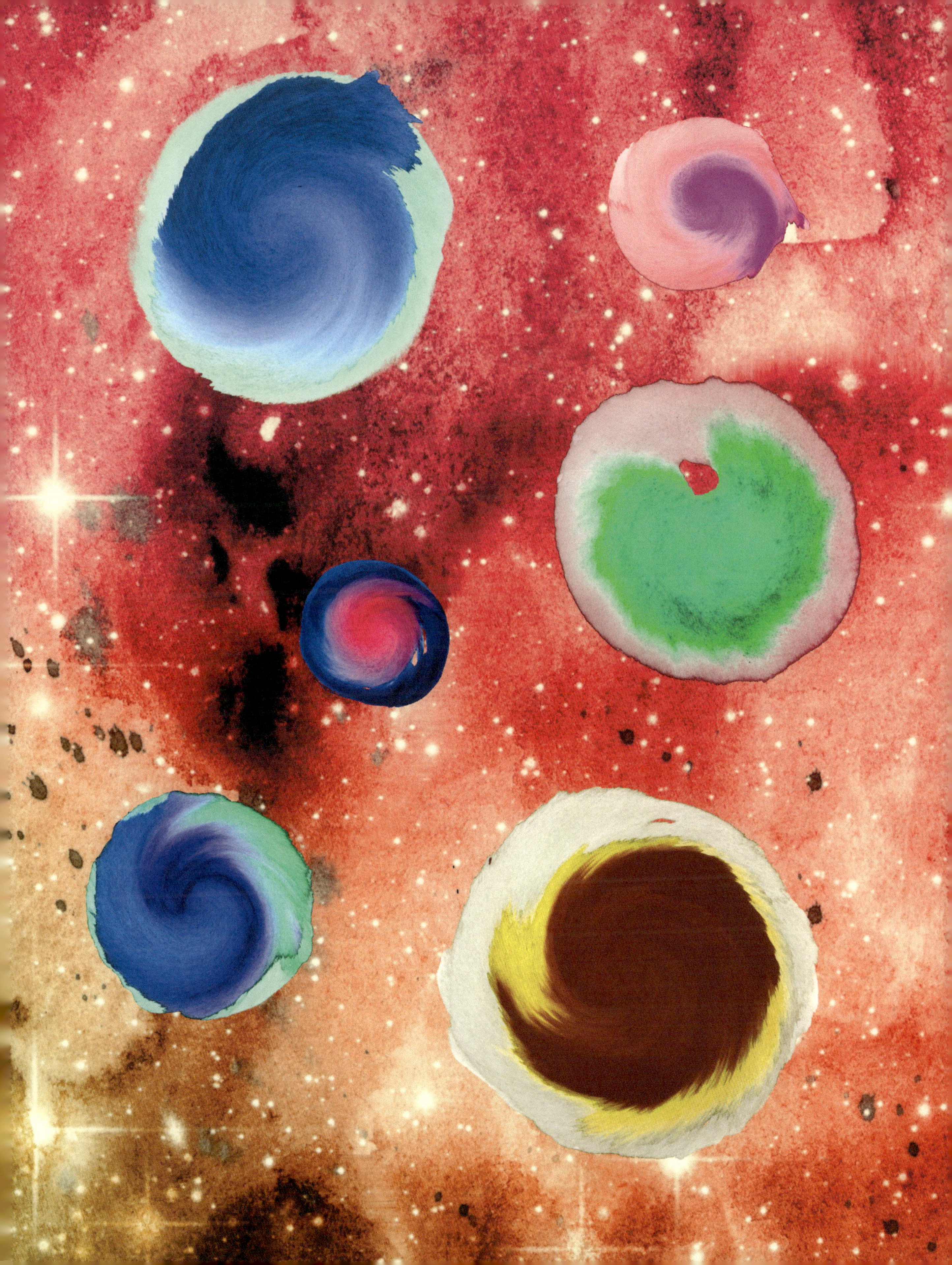

BLANK PAGE

CAN YOU IMAGINE THE SPACE BETWEEN YOUR TOP AND BOTTOM LIP?

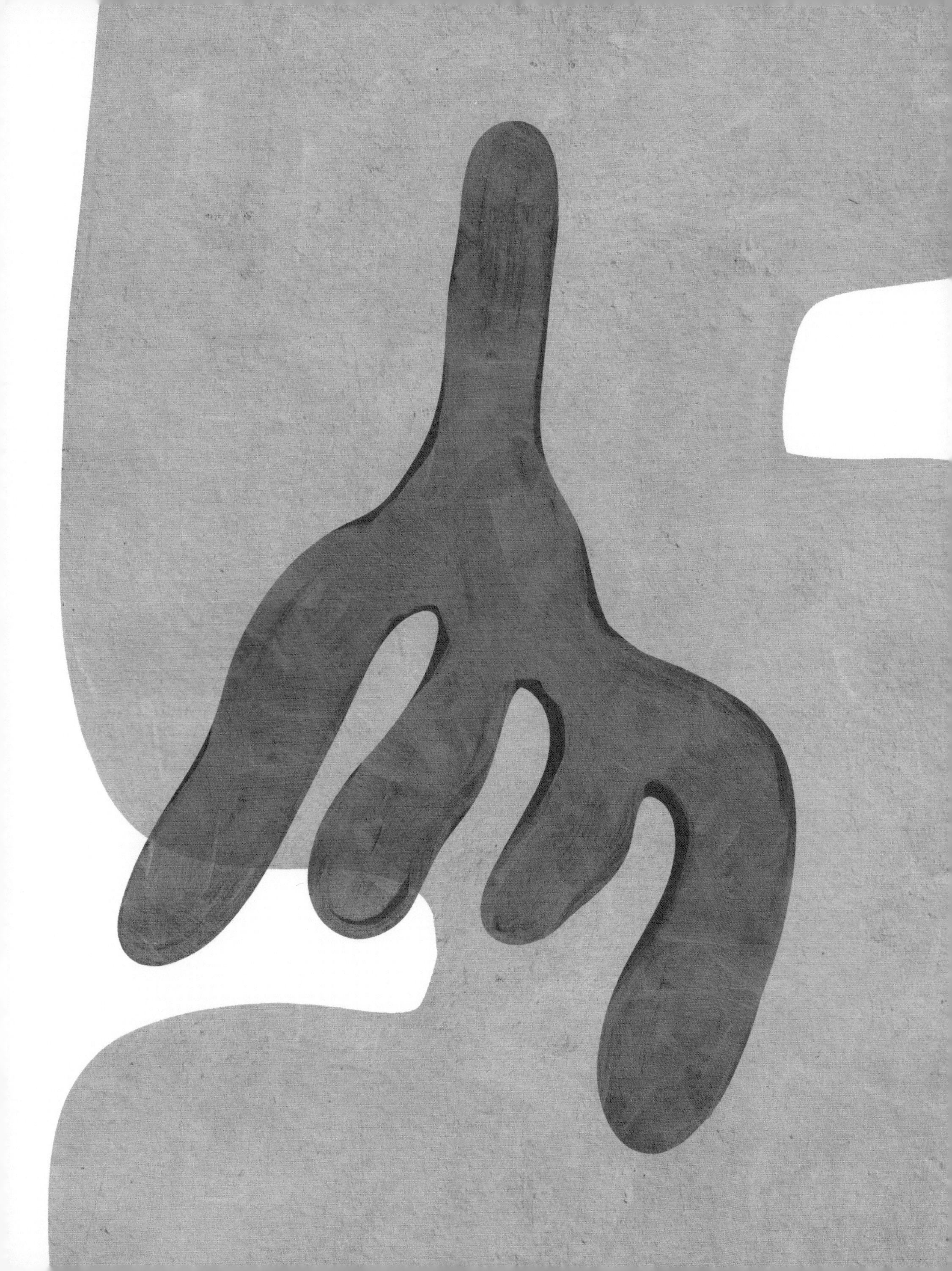

BLANK PAGE

WHAT DOES YOUR HEART BEAT FEEL LIKE?

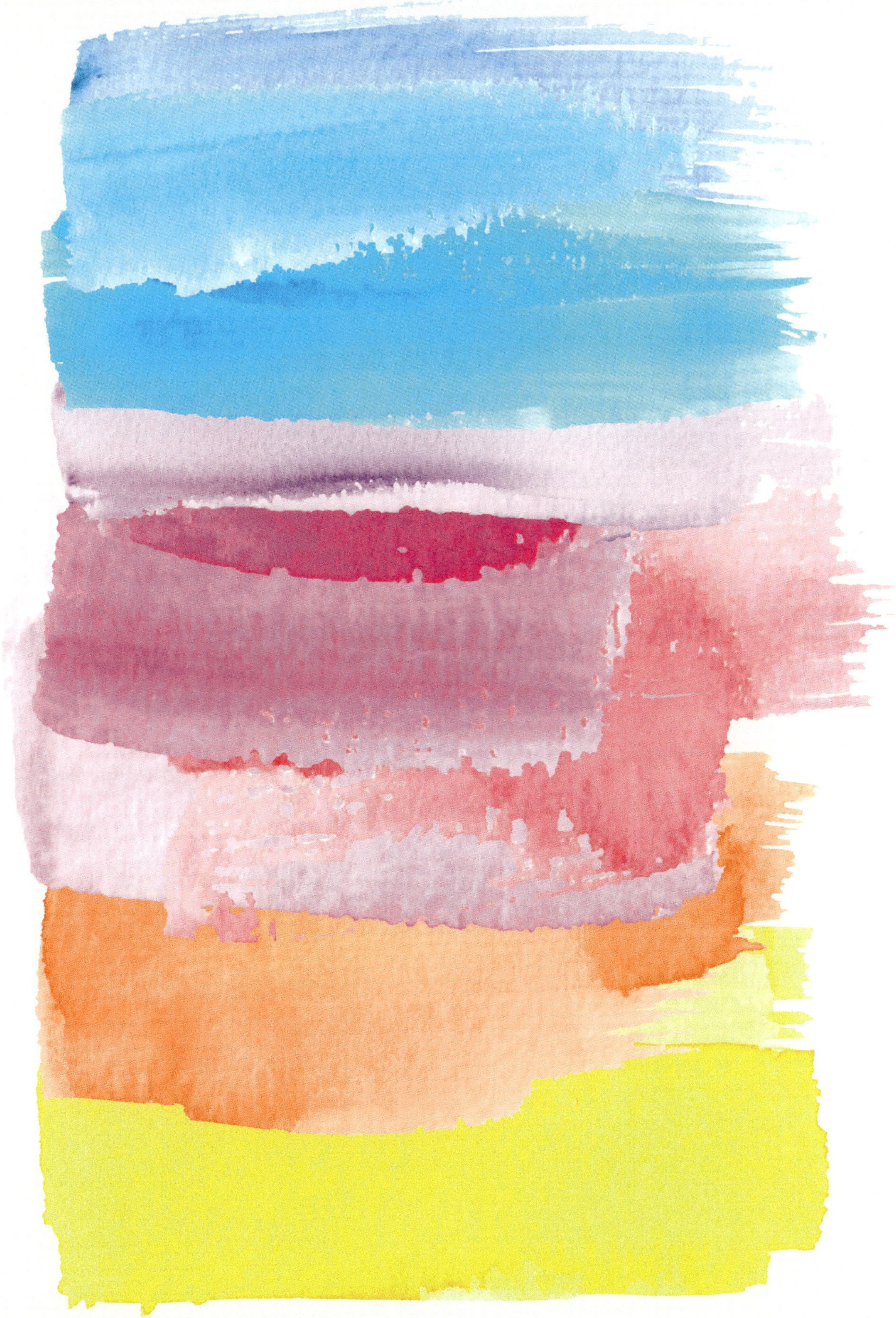

BLANK PAGE

IF YOU COULD CHANGE ONE THING WHAT WOULD IT BE?

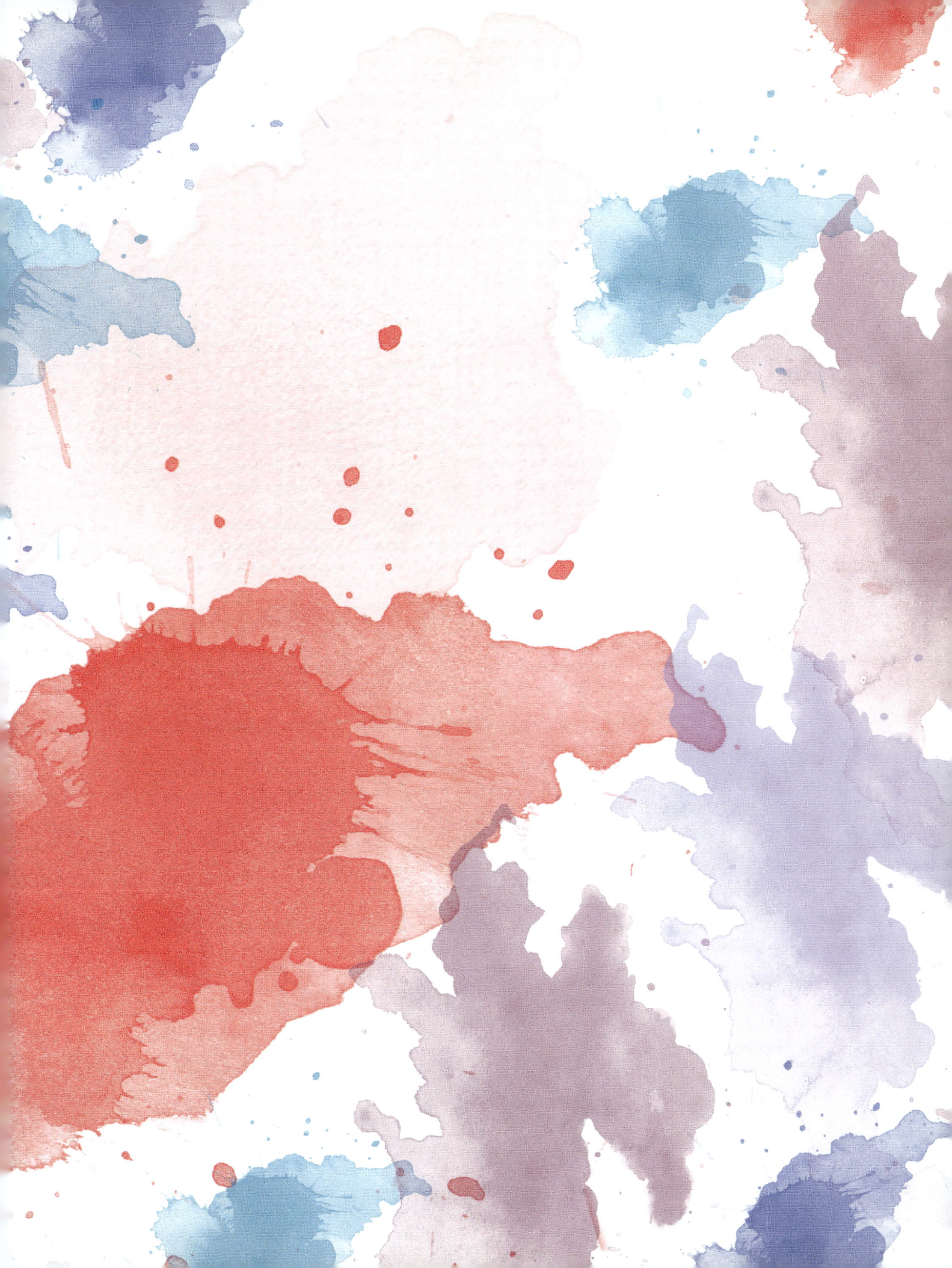

BLANK PAGE

WHAT INSPIRES YOU?

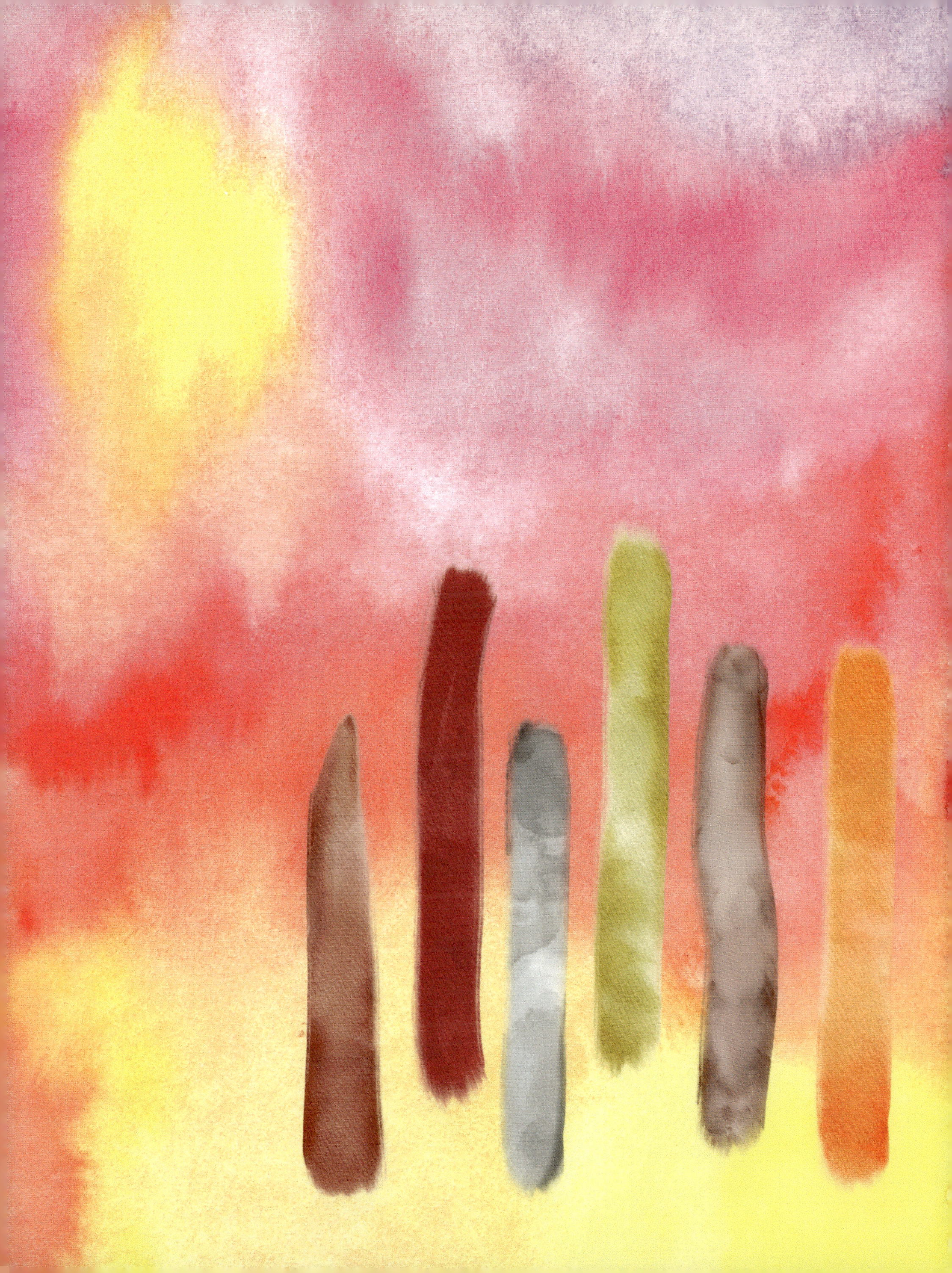

BLANK PAGE

CAN YOU IMAGINE THE SPACE BETWEEN YOUR HEART AND YOUR SPINE?

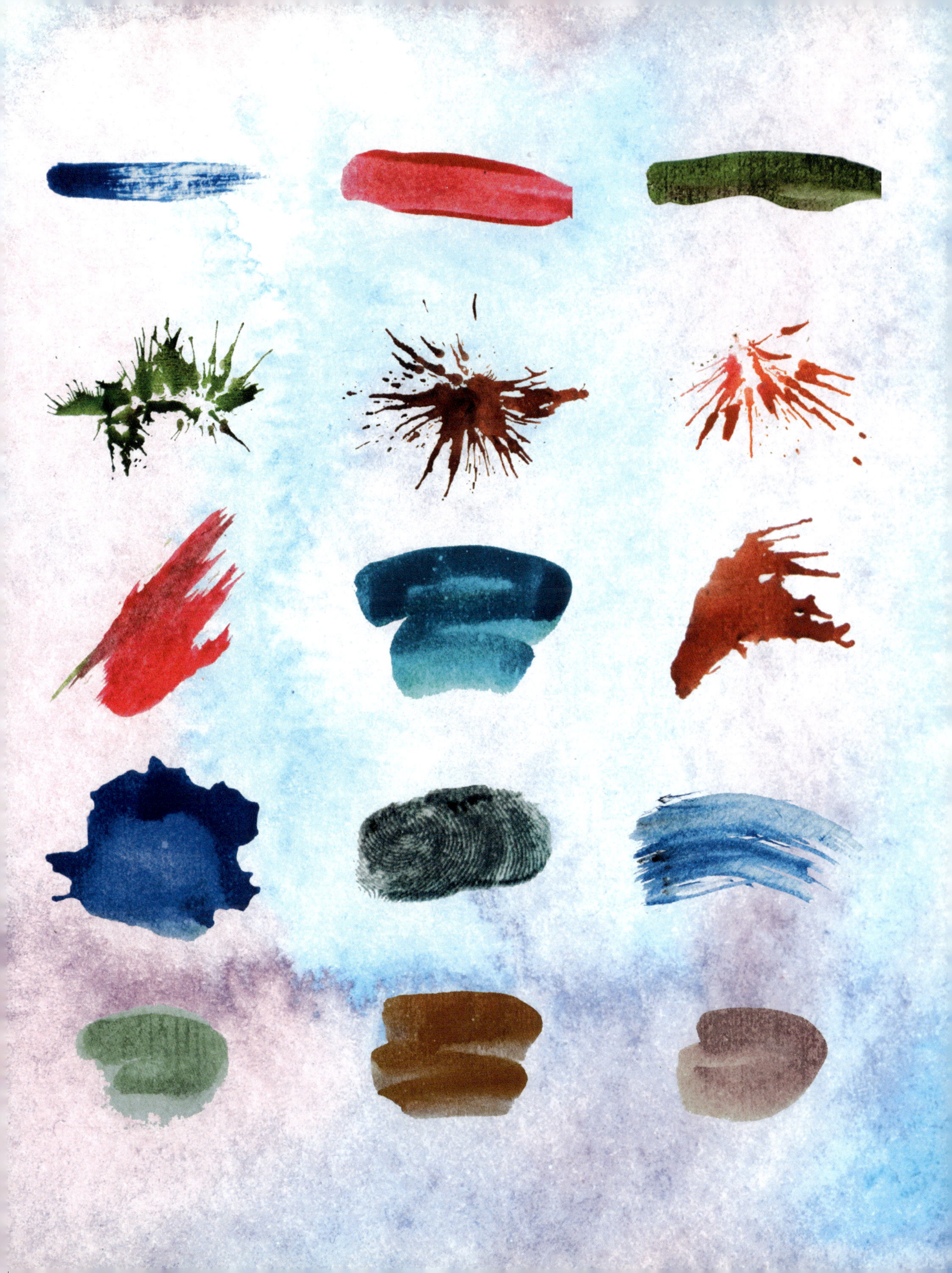

BLANK PAGE

WHAT ARE YOU THANKFUL FOR?

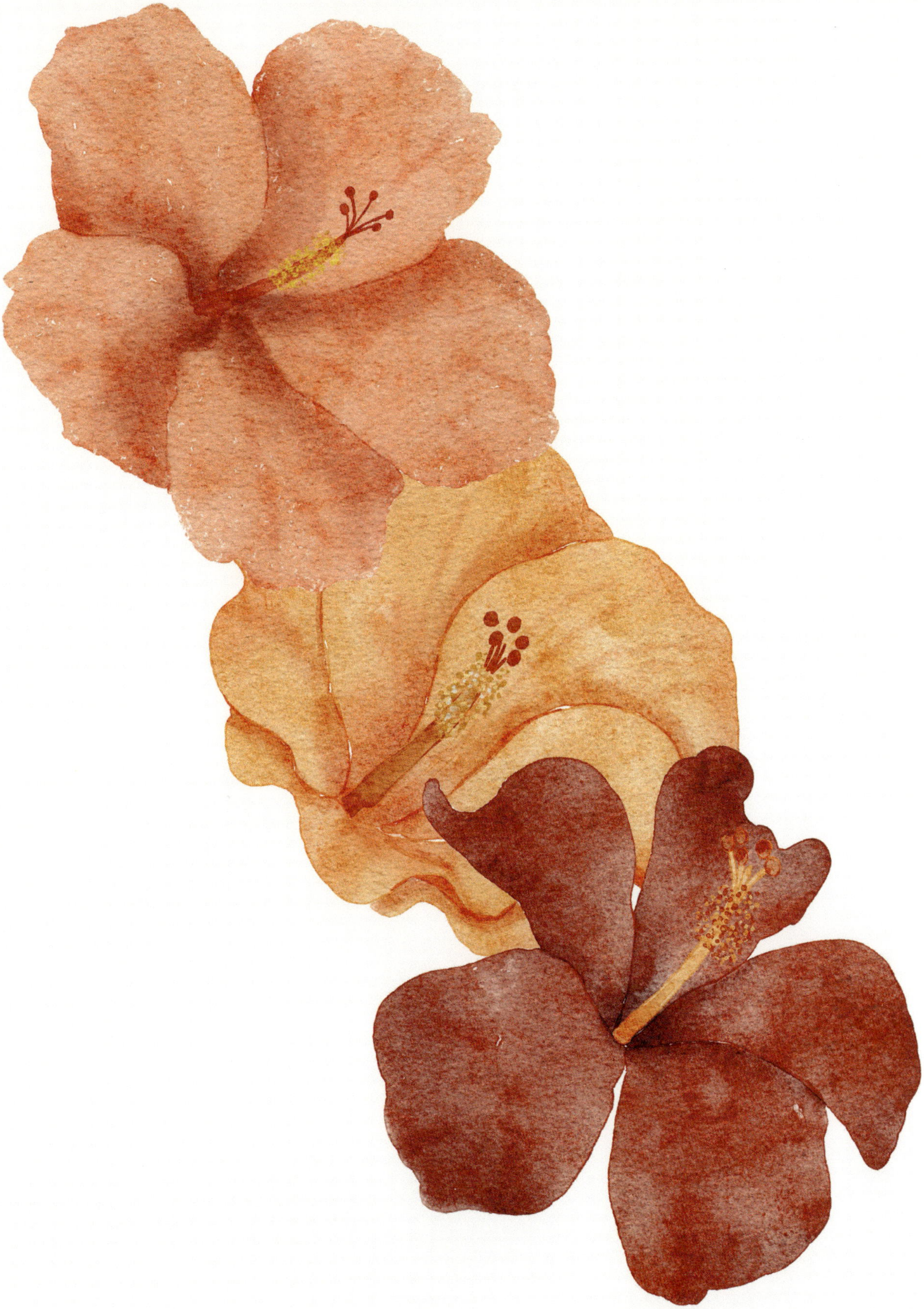

BLANK PAGE

IS THERE ONE THING YOU WOULD WANT A SECOND CHANCE WITH?

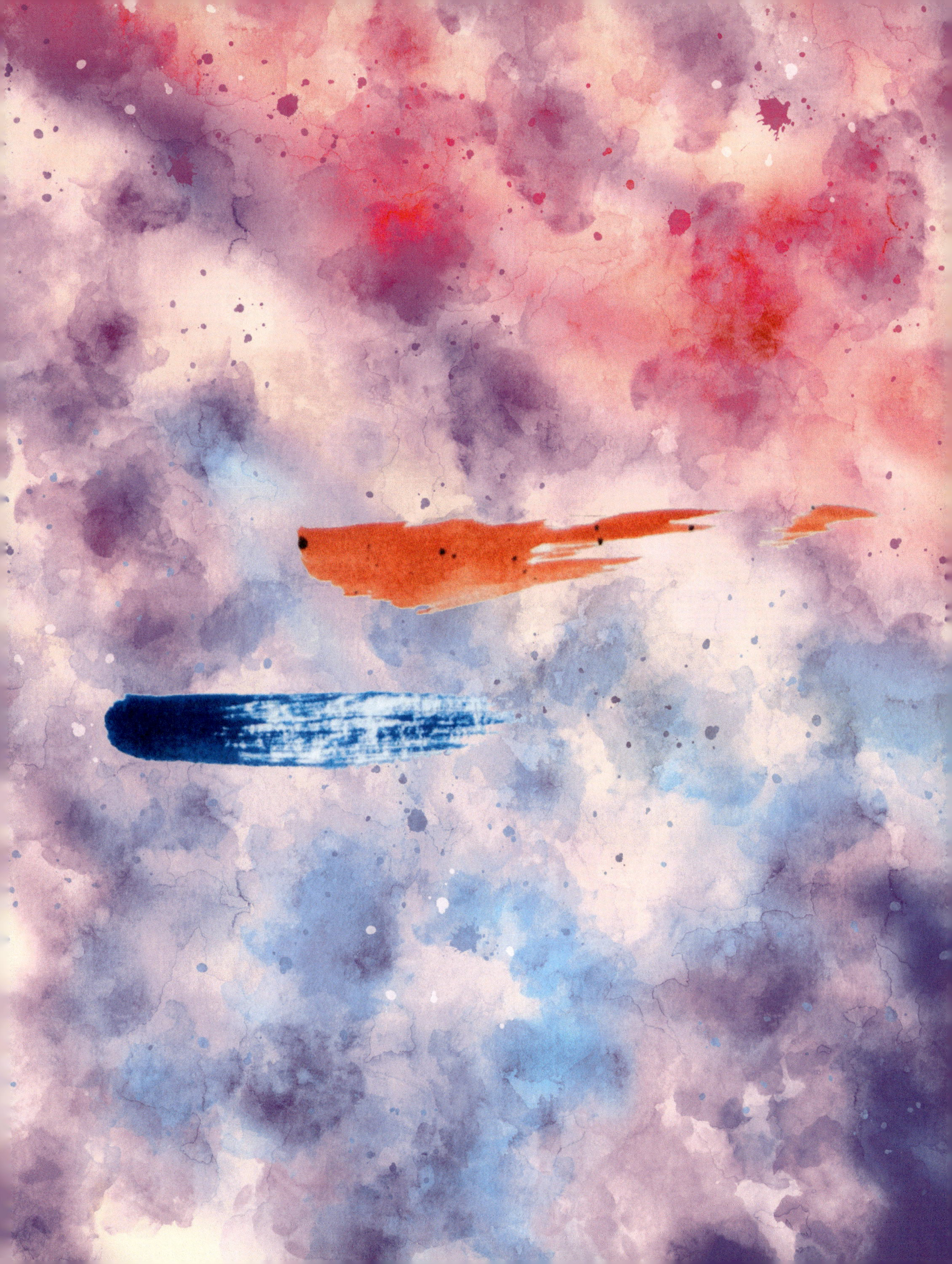

BLANK PAGE

IS THERE ONE THING YOU WANT TO LET GO OF?

BLANK PAGE

HOW DO YOU SHOW YOUR EMOTIONS?

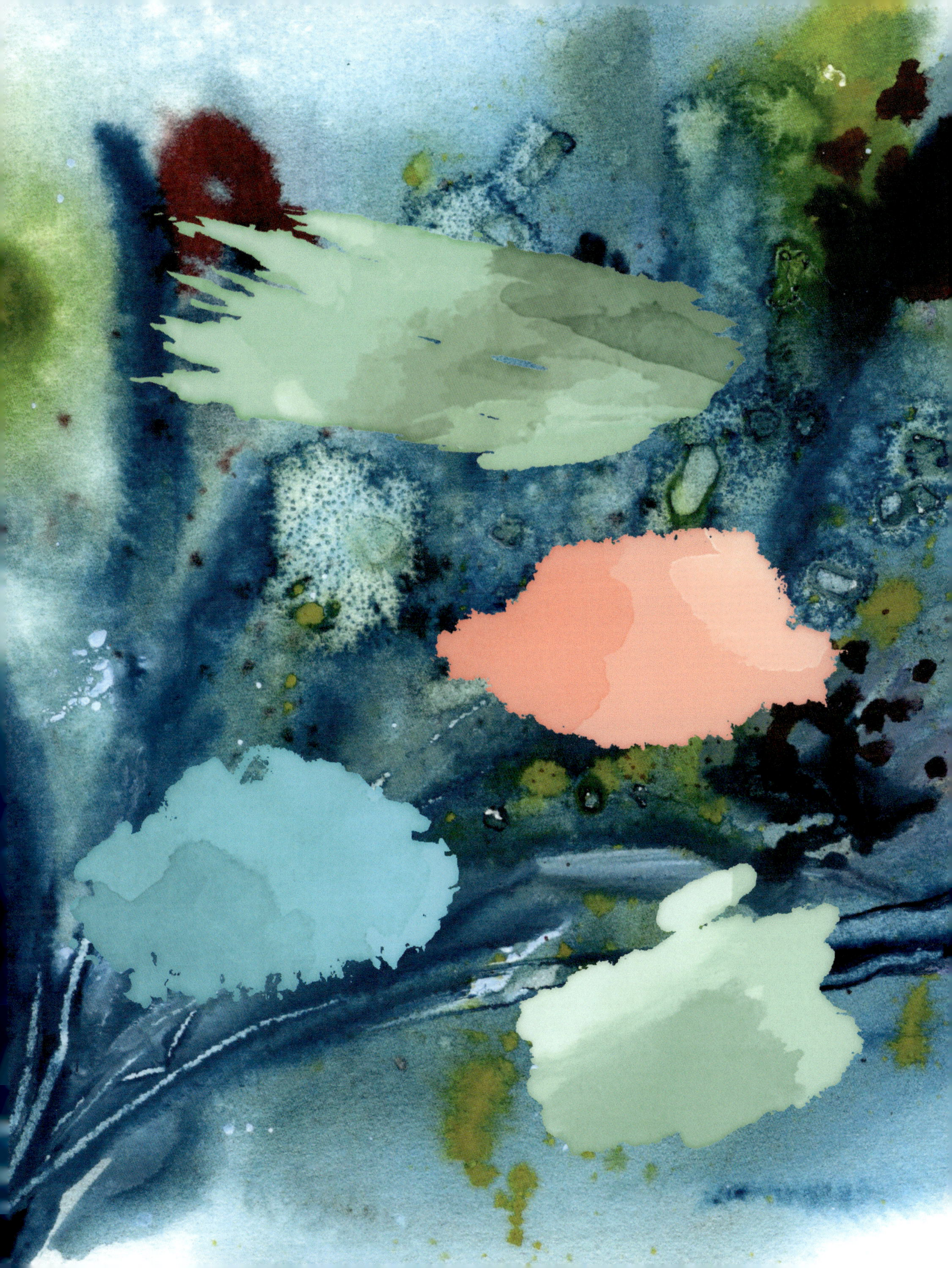

BLANK PAGE

DO YOU EVER FEEL LOST?

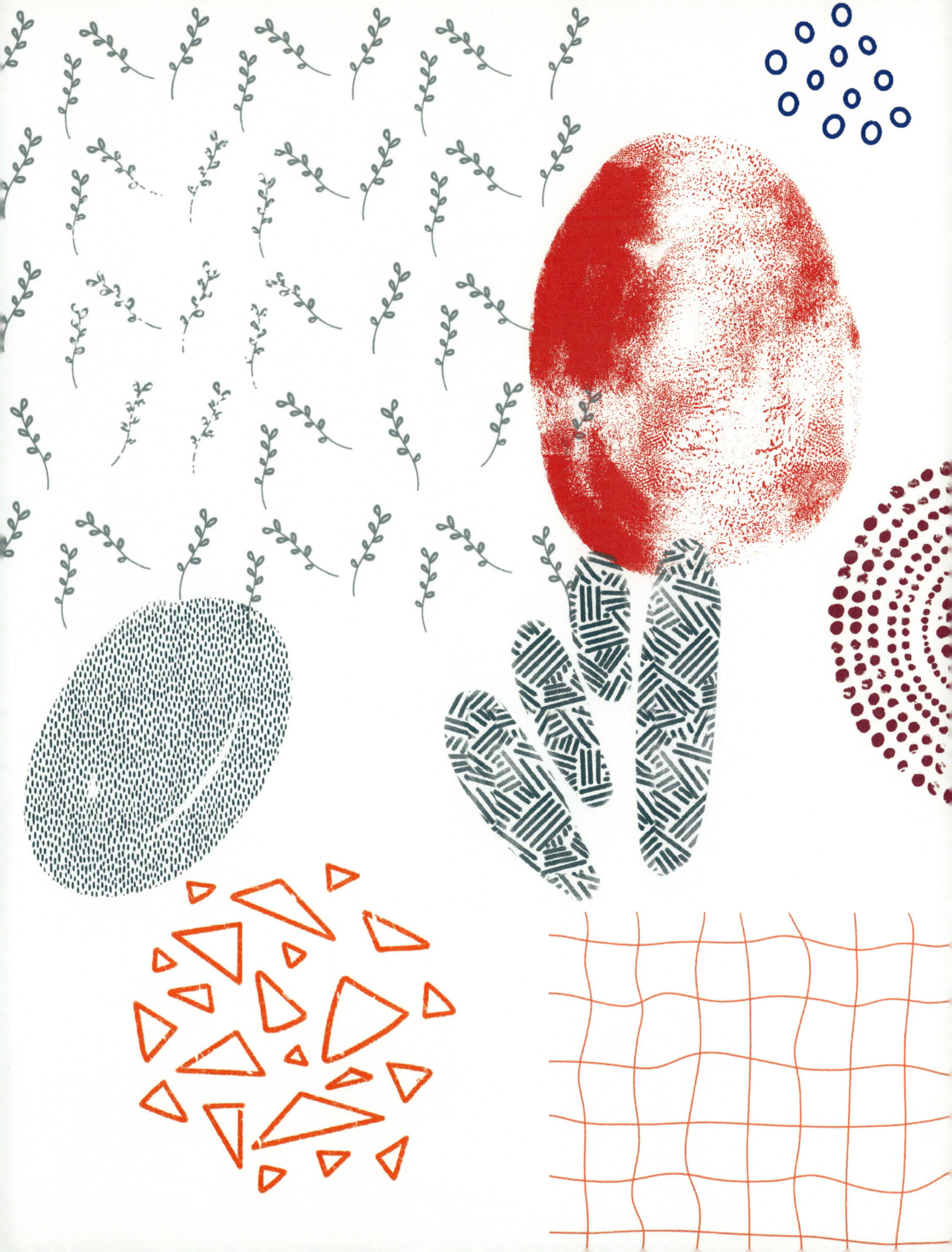

BLANK PAGE

CAN YOU IMAGINE THE SPACE BETWEEN YOUR RIGHT HIP AND LEFT HIP?

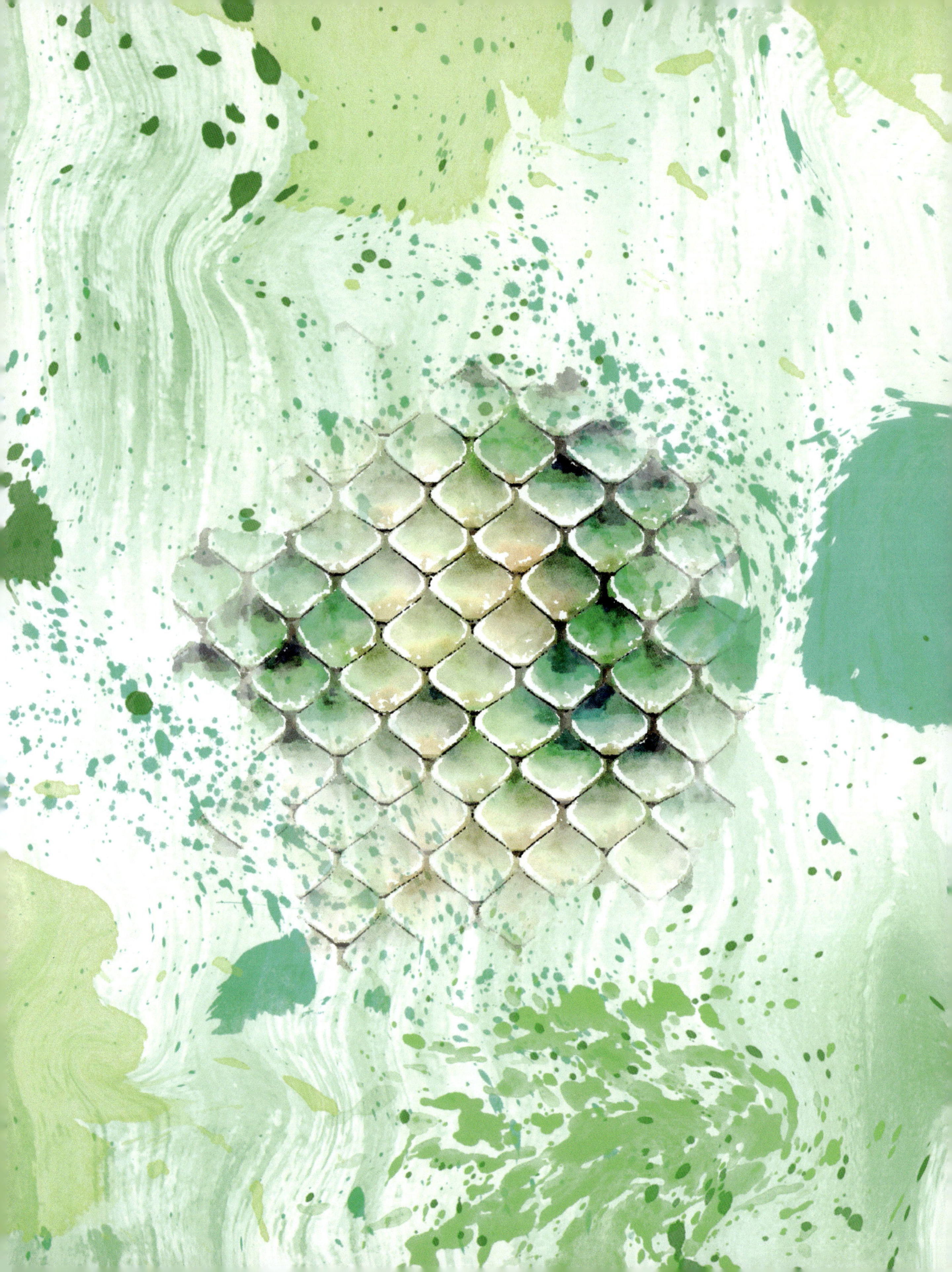

BLANK PAGE

WHAT WAS THE BIGGEST EVENT IN YOUR LIFE SO FAR?

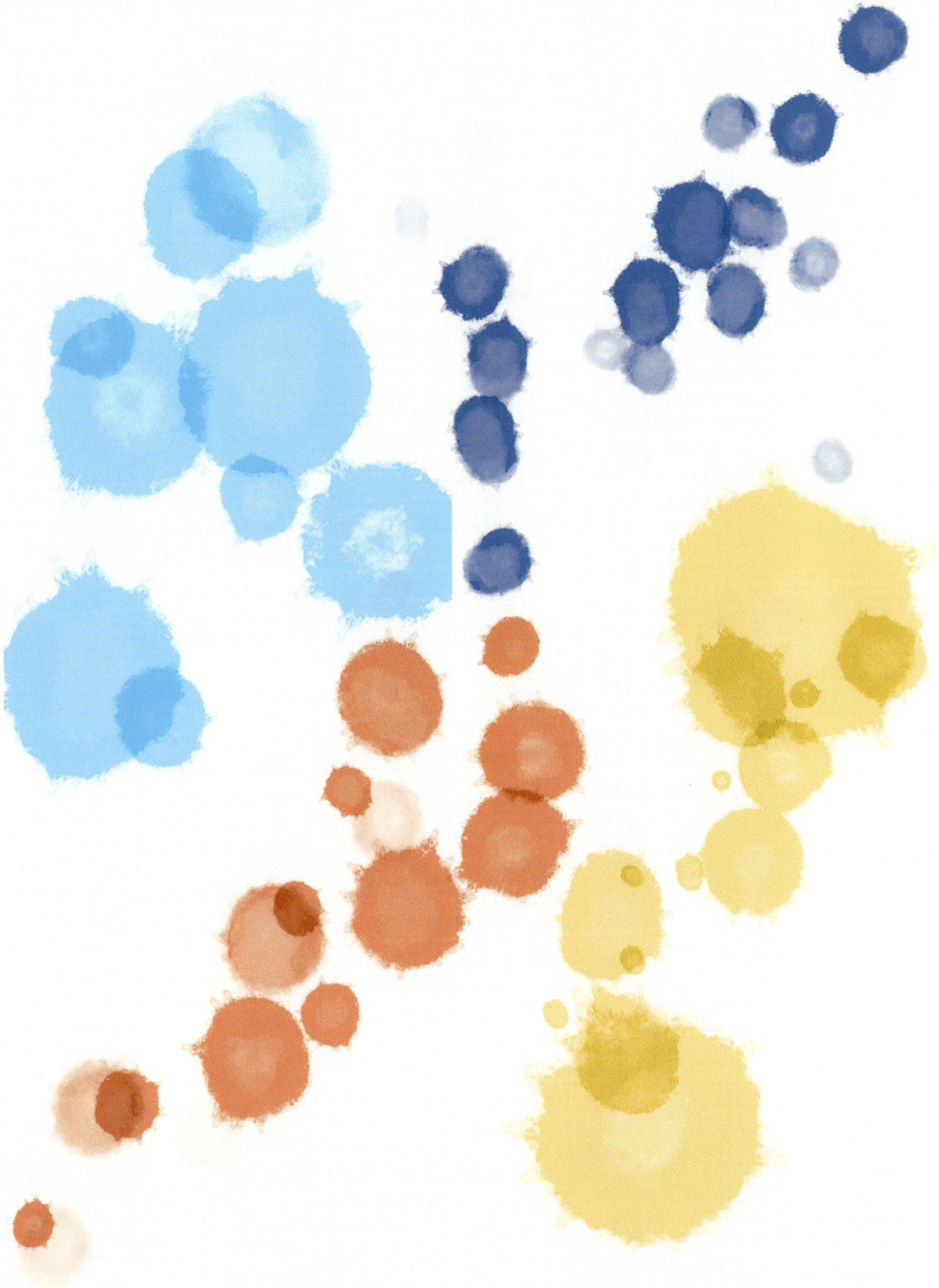

BLANK PAGE

DO YOU HAVE A BIGGEST REGRET?

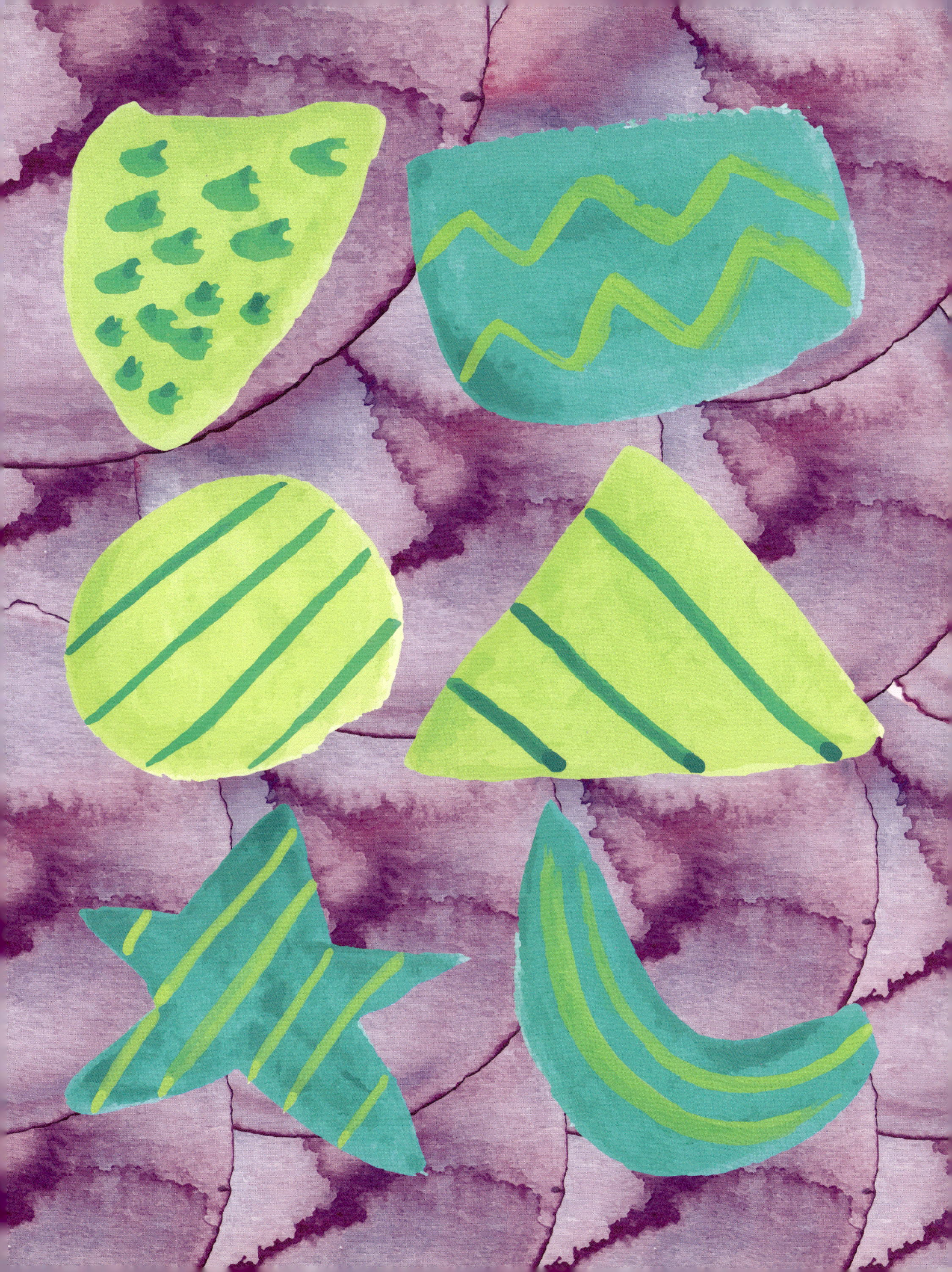

BLANK PAGE

HOW DO YOU MEASURE SUCCESS?

BLANK PAGE

WHAT DO YOU THINK YOU ARE REALLY GOOD AT?

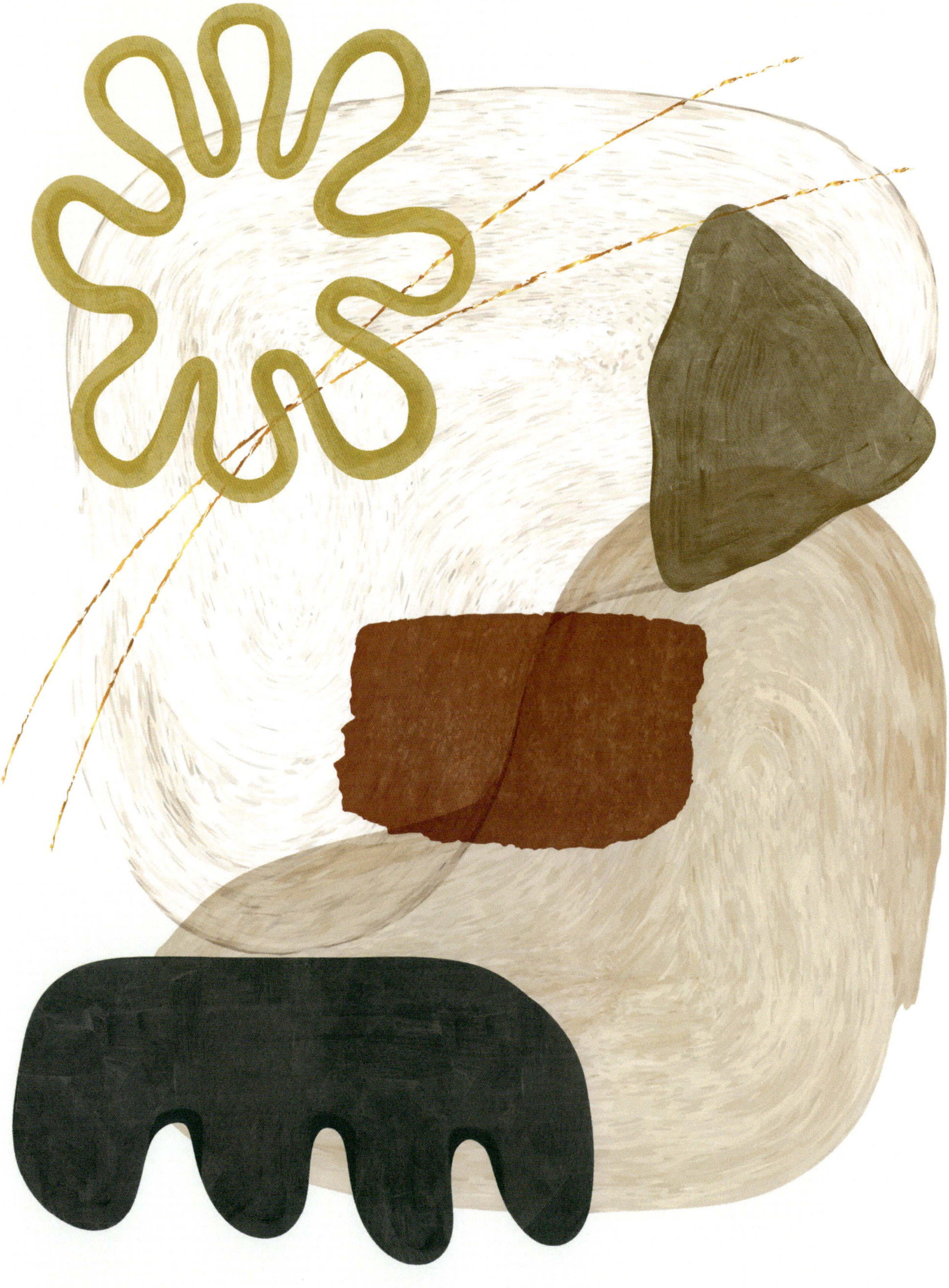

BLANK PAGE

CAN YOU IMAGINE THE SPACE BETWEEN YOUR HEART AND YOUR STOMACH?

BLANK PAGE

WHAT DO YOU THINK MAKES LIFE MEANINGFUL?

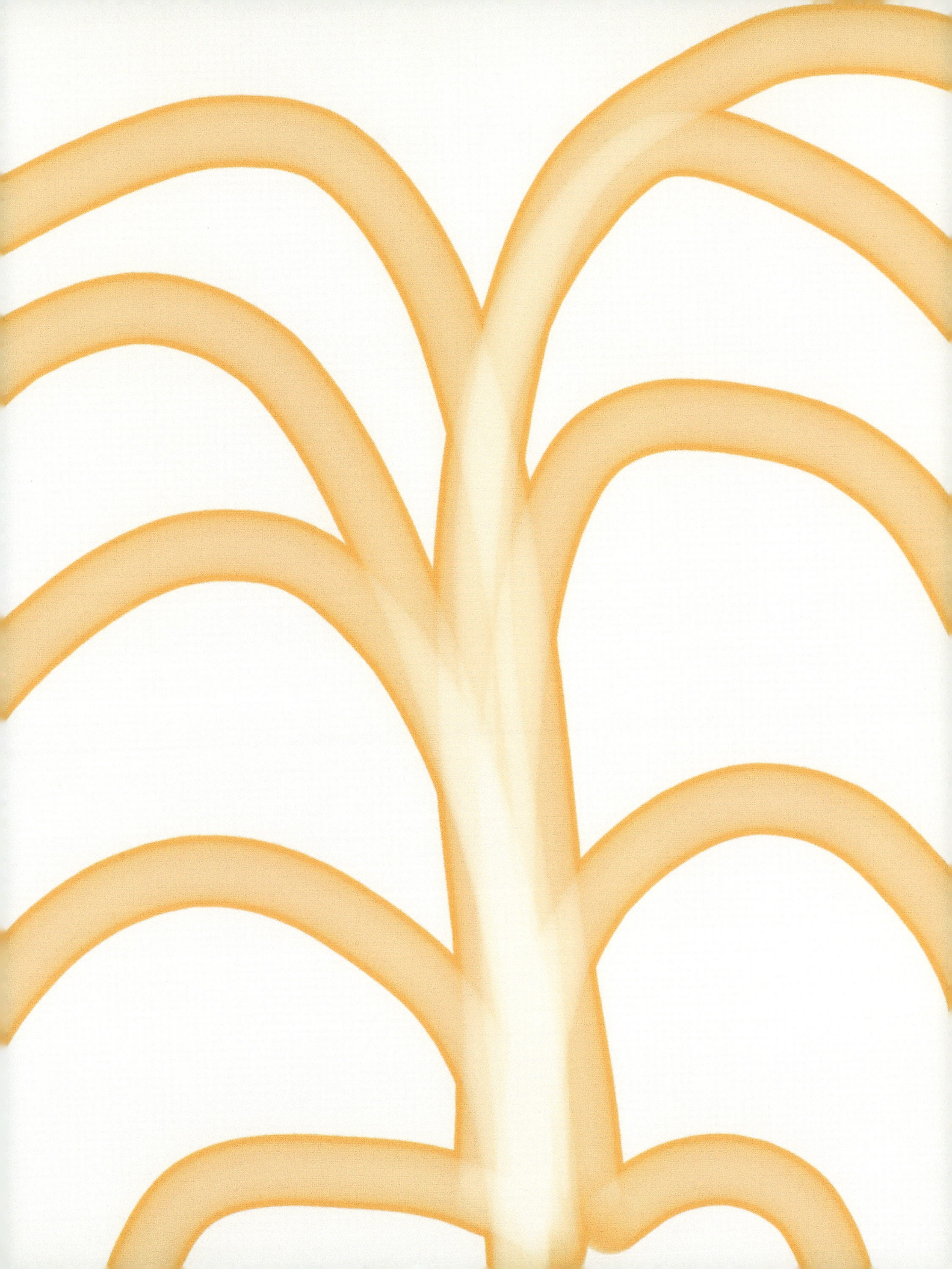

BLANK PAGE

IS THERE ANYTHING HOLDING YOU BACK IN LIFE?

BLANK PAGE

CAN YOU IMAGINE THE ENTIRE VOLUME OF YOUR CHEST?

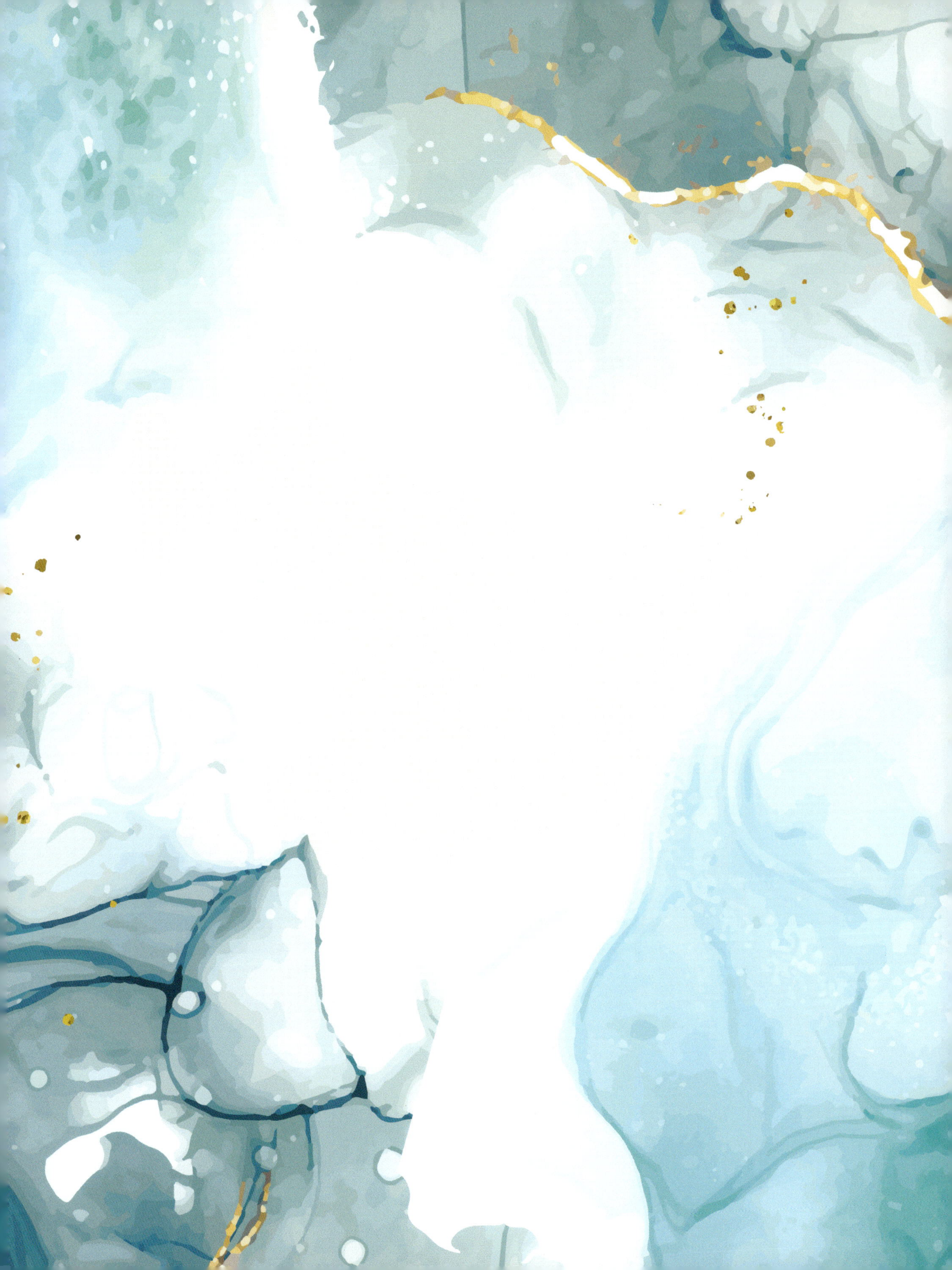

BLANK PAGE

WHAT GIVES YOU MOTIVATION?

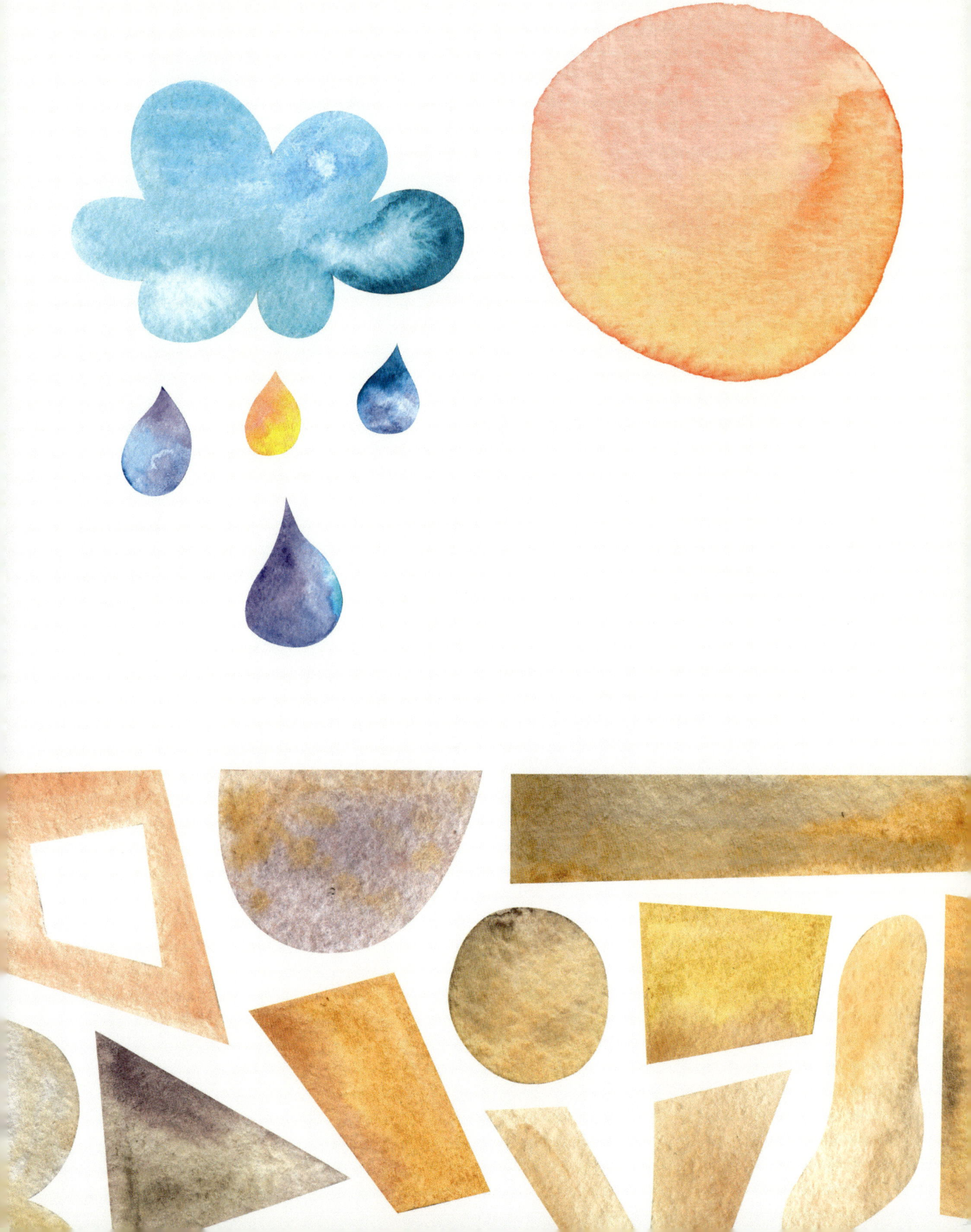

BLANK PAGE

WHAT OPPORTUNITIES ARE YOU LOOKING FOR IN THE FUTURE?

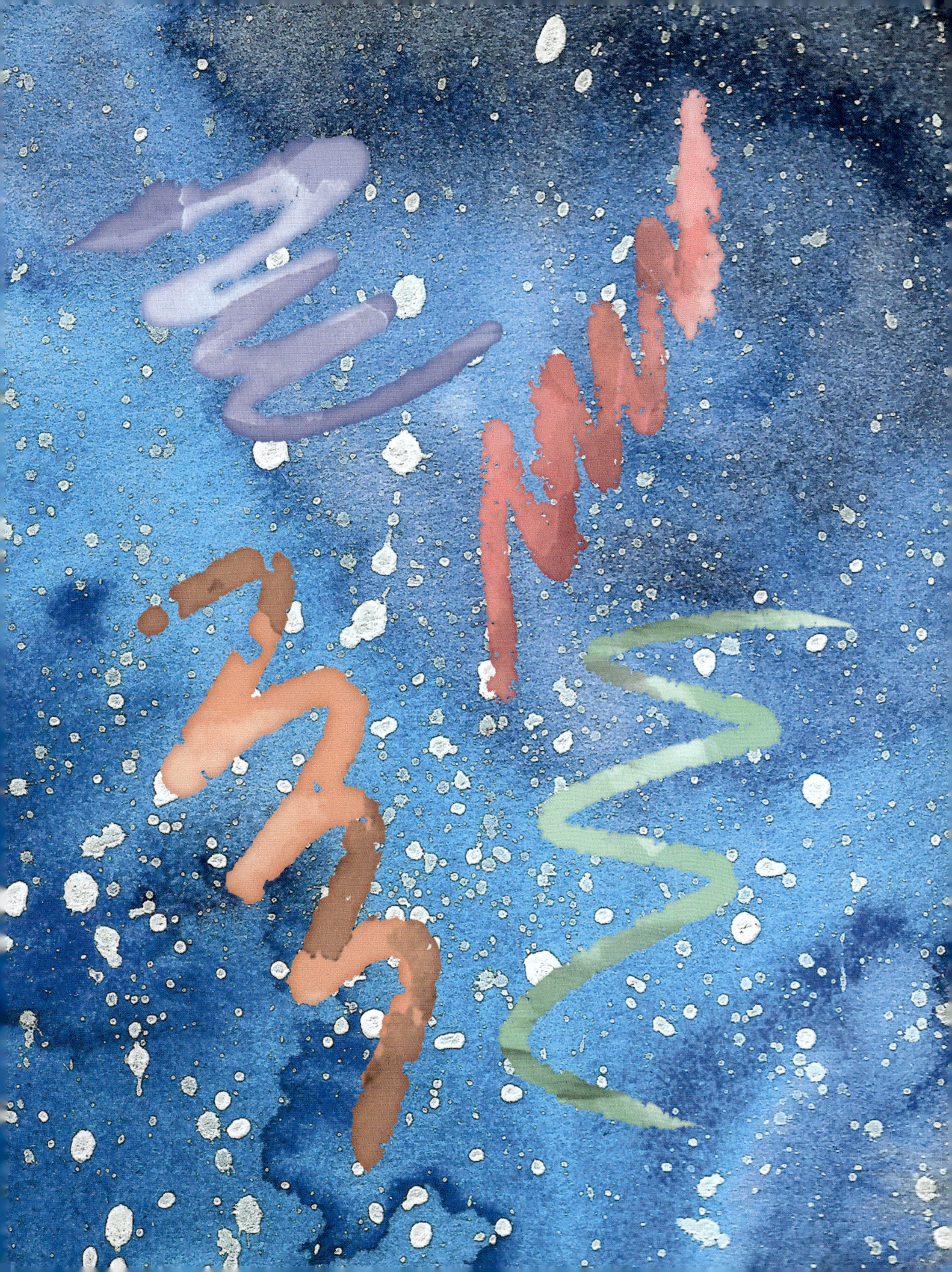

BLANK PAGE

WHAT THINGS MAKE YOU LOSE TRACK OF TIME?

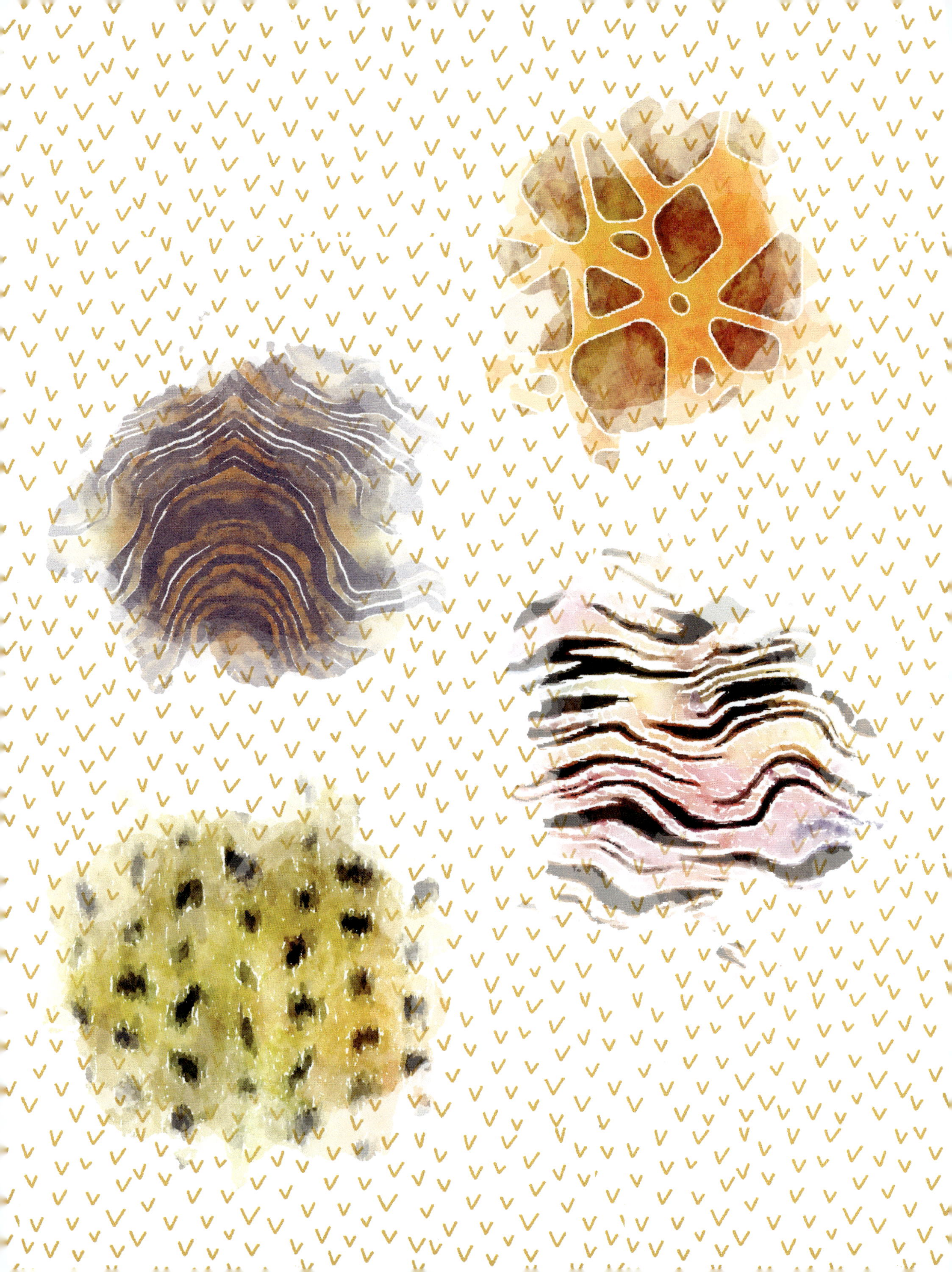

BLANK PAGE

HOW DO YOU FEEL RIGHT NOW?

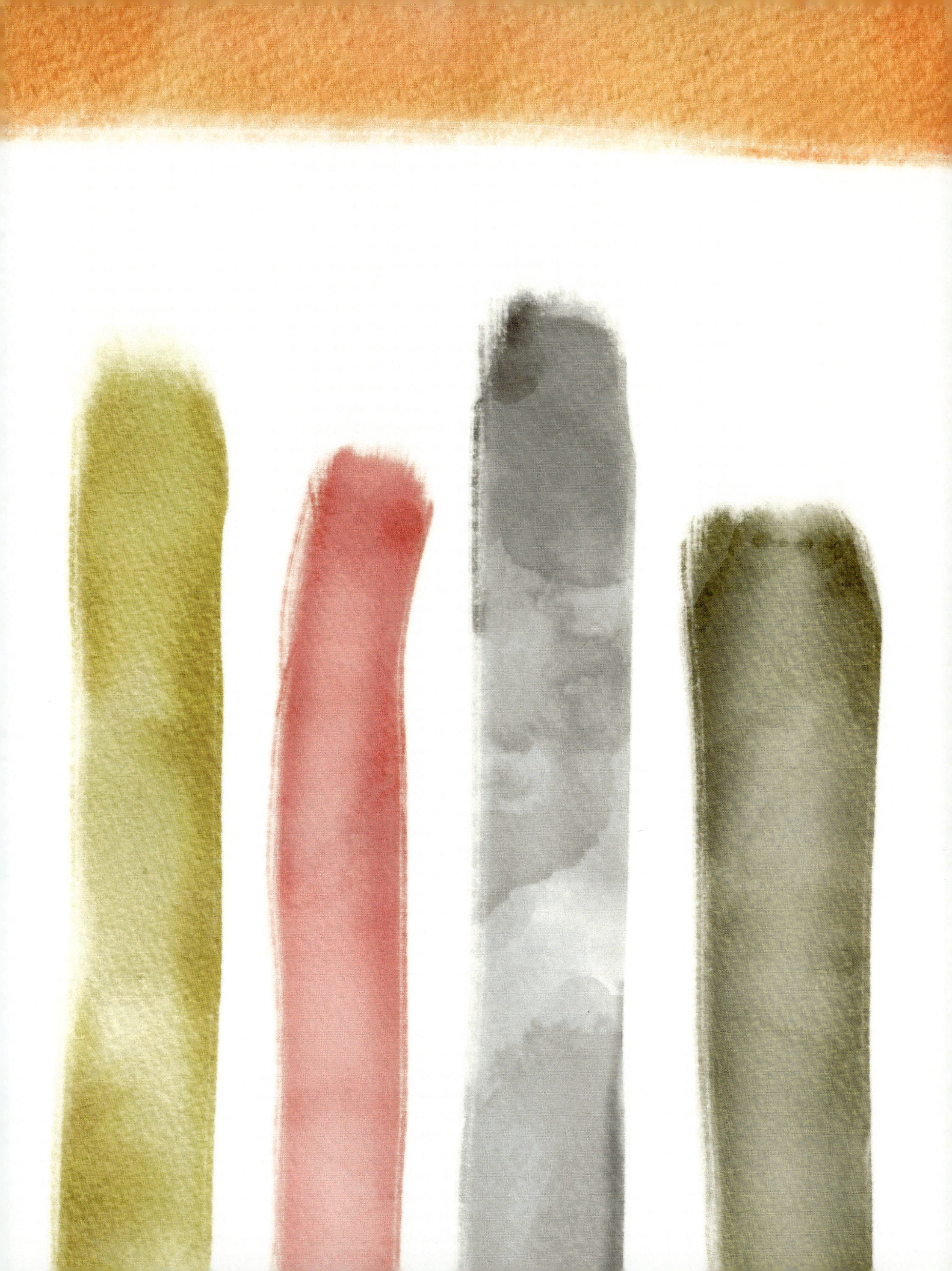

Printed in Great Britain
by Amazon